TOXIC!

Endorsement

It is an incredibly honest book. I finally get what people say about a book being "gripping." I held a good grip on the book, not wanting to put it down. I read it in two days. I had to know how things looked once you were on the other side of the wolf. It gripped my mind because I felt like I was there, a fly on the wall in each room you described. I ignored the room (and people!) around me, engrossed in your story. I went to sleep feeling concerned for Beth, having read the first half. Then I woke up feeling very relieved because there was still half a book of growth and sharing left. I loved how you wrapped it all together in the end.

I loved one chapter ending in the book because I flipped the page, and there was just one line that added a whole new angle to everything. It pulled me sideways in one sentence, adding a depth I wasn't expecting.

I wish I could be as brave as you in owning my hard truths. We should all be so clear, so ready to share, and so compelling in the forgiveness of self. I feel like you are an artist who has sketched a picture using darkness and light to create a portrait of overcoming.

Suzette Hamblin

TOXIC!

The Big Bad Wolf is NOT a Fairy Tale!

ELIZABETH BROWN

Goodyear, Arizona

First published in the USA in 2022 by Elizabeth Brown

Note: The author is Canadian, so Canadian spelling is used in this book.

Publisher: Becky Norwood, Spotlight Publishing House™
https://SpotlightPublishingHouse.com
Editor: Lynn Thompson, Living on Purpose Communications
Book Cover: Lalnspiratriz (stock.adobe.com)
Cover Designer: Angie Alaya
Interior Design: Marigold2k

DISCLAIMER

eBook ISBN: 978-1-958405-22-2
Paperback ISBN: 978-1-958405-23-9

Dedication

To My Family

Thank you for all your love and
support throughout the years!

To The Healers who have helped
to restore my sanity,
I couldn't have done it without you!

To All Women who have walked the same
treacherous path I did,

May you grow in strength, wisdom,
and self-compassion.

Contents

Foreword

In *TOXIC! The Big Bad Wolf is NOT a Fairy Tale,* author Elizabeth Brown reveals what made her wait decades before uncovering the details of her story. It took tremendous strength, courage, and heart conviction for her to share her experiences finally—all the while keeping me riveted to my chair.

I have known Elizabeth for about two decades. I knew her when she first wanted to write this book, and we met again a few years ago when she asked me to be her writing coach; she was ready to tell the tale. Working with Elizabeth has been a true delight—a privilege to walk beside someone who rewrote a story of abuse to live fully today—free from the pain of the past when her young life was left shattered.

Elizabeth is now free from anger, shame, guilt, and blame after taking a hero's journey to transformation and transcendence. Today she easily holds compassion for herself, her predator, and all the others who have hurt her. She tells her story with candid descriptions laden with retrospective insight and humour that had me laughing out loud.

Elizabeth's motivation for writing this book was to settle her mind, and as she expressed on many occasions, "Junie, if I can prevent one person from being abused this way or help them to leave and not look back, my journey has been worthwhile."

As a woman once involved with a Big Bad Wolf, aka a man who sought to control me through cunning and deceit, I understand how it results in confusion, self-hatred, heart-ache, and post-traumatic stress disorder. But unfortunately, I lived in denial for a long time rather than facing the truth.

Do you feel that you are in an abusive relationship? Are you thinking of leaving your abuser? Take the time to read Elizabeth's book cover to cover for helpful insights, guidance, and encouragement on your journey.

Junie Swadron
Psychotherapist and book-writing coach
Author of *Re-Write Your Life* and *Your Life Matters*
www.junieswadron.com

Introduction

A rose is a rose by any other name, and a Big Bad Wolf is a Big Bad Wolf by any other moniker. I can call him a villain, a snake, a narcissist; whatever name I call my wolf, it doesn't take an expert to see that our relationship was TOXIC!

Paul, a social services counsellor, presented himself to our family as a sensitive, spiritual man, unselfishly devoting his life to helping those in need.

When I met him, Paul told me he studied with an Indigenous shaman and had psychic and healing powers.

My mother was also smitten with him; however, she did not know about our secret relationship. Being young, inexperienced, and far easier to manipulate, I was the one he chose. He was so charming and encouraging of me; he seemed to get me as a person. My relationship with God was of utmost importance to me, and it seemed that it was also a priority to him.

Paul never beat me or hurled ugly names at me. He never put me down in front of other people or cheated me out of my money. Instead, he used deceit and manipulation to gain control of me emotionally, spiritually, and psychically slowly but surely to the point where I hardly knew who I was anymore. In the fourteen months that I was with Paul, I went from being a confident and optimistic young woman to a shadow of my former self. His influence ruined almost every aspect of my life. It took me years to find the help I needed to recover.

Finally, half a century later, I can share my story. I could not do so earlier. For one thing, I felt ashamed about becoming involved with a man who was married and 34 years older than me. I wondered if my readers would think I was immoral and deserved the dire consequences. Indeed, I thought that of myself.

I first thought of writing this book in 1999 and finished a rough draft. What stopped me? I looked at myself and thought, *yes, I've been through a lot of therapy,* but I still struggled with depression, anxiety, and issues around food; plus, I was unsure how my husband (now late) would feel about the sudden exposure to my murky past. Also, I didn't want to hurt my family or Paul's remaining family members.

Now, it's 2022, and I'm still dealing with stuff. However, it occurred to me that this book would never get written if I kept worrying about reaching total emotional and spiritual enlightenment. So, currently, my motto is "progress, not perfection." Although I'm far from perfect, I am enjoying my life.

If you are or have been involved in a toxic relationship and taken advantage of by a deceiver and manipulator, it is my wish that you do not feel isolated. A minister once told me, "If you ever find yourself in hell, keep walking!" Don't give up. So many more resources are available now than fifty years ago. Keep walking, avail yourself of all the help you can get, and eventually, you'll find that life can be beautiful again.

Although most of the people in my narrative have passed away, I have changed the names of my family and other people involved. This story is true.

1

Post-War

My mom took part in the Warsaw Uprising. The post-war photos of her formerly beautiful city, once known as the Paris of the East, show its utter ruin. The bombing reduced ninety percent of the city to a heap of rubble—bricks, wood, mortar—leaving its half-starved citizens with the almost hopeless task of rebuilding Poland's capital and cultural center.

My soul was like that—post-Paul. In the brief time I was involved with this man, my charismatic ex-counsellor, psychic, shaman, and lover, I felt like a burned-out, bombed-out shell with nothing left inside but blackness, bleakness, and a sense of doom. Frightening urges and images swirled like ugly cesspools in my overwrought psyche. Food became an unholy significance for me, and I ate and ate and ate to bursting. It was too much; it was all too much. I had to get rid of my psychic and physical overload. "Bulimia," the act of purging food immediately after eating, either by laxative or throwing up, was not commonly spoken or written about in the 1970s, nor was the term "post-traumatic stress." I thought I was mad.

When I was 21 years old, I had the chance to visit Warsaw. Taking in the tall buildings and the wide boulevards lined with beautiful trees and parks, I would never have known there was a war—they restored the *Stare Miasto* (old town) to its former medieval glory. Indeed, there was a glorious resurrection, but at what price and by what sacrificial effort of the previous generation?

After Paul, I had to rebuild my inner city, too, which would take a long time, but now, I am here to tell the story.

2

Three Cautionary Tales

Before I jump into my journey of dealing with and healing from psychic and emotional manipulation, I would like to share three stories. Myths and fairy tales often contain hard truths about what makes our psyches tick and makes us vulnerable to those who trick us. They show us the story behind the story. I believe that the tales of *Red Riding Hood, Echo and Narcissus,* and *The Emperor's New Clothes* will help the reader understand the nature of a dysfunctional relationship and why it can be so difficult to recognize and speak our inner truth.

Red Riding Hood (with a twist)

Once upon a time, there was a Big Bad Wolf. He didn't think he was a bad fellow, simply a guy trying to get through the hardscrabble of life. If he ingested a few people along the way, well, it was their fault for wandering alone into the dark, dense forest, his home. Besides, they were tastier than his usual fare and far easier to catch.

For several years, he'd seen the little girl playing on the edge of the forest. She did not interest him, such a scrawny, skinny little thing she was. He never bothered with her; it would be like eating a bird. Hardly worth it! However, one day, there she was, wearing a red velvet hood, carrying a basket into the woods. It seemed she had ripened into a plump, juicy, succulent young maiden almost overnight. Mm mm! He smacked his lips and set forth after her. But wait! What was in her basket? More food, perhaps? And who was she going to visit? Could he maybe get two meals for the price of one? He needed to find out more.

He was looking good that day after feasting on a wealthy merchant a few nights earlier and obtaining a beautifully embroidered white tuxedo, a paisley tie, and a pair of kick-ass blue suede shoes. Confidently he caught up with the young woman.

"Well, hello there, doll!" He bowed politely. "My, my, my! Aren't you a beauty? Why, you look good enough to eat!"

Red fluttered her mascaraed eyelashes and giggled. (She'd stolen the mascara from her mother; she wasn't supposed to wear it.) She licked her illicitly lip-sticked lips.

"Might I ask where a fine young lady might be going on an evening such as this?"

"I'm off to see Granny. She's not feeling well. Mom gave me food and potions to take to her. I'm not supposed to go through here, but I missed the Number 43 bus, and it's getting late, so I figured I'd take a shortcut. Her cottage is straight ahead a few kilometres."

"That might not be the safest route. Might I accompany you?"

"No, Granny wouldn't approve. I'm not even supposed to be talking to you. Besides, I have a flashlight which I can also use as a weapon."

"Ah," said the wolf, undeterred. "Then I shall be on my way. Stay safe, fair maiden." Now that he knew the loca-

tion, he would reach Grandma's cottage long before Red was due to make her appearance. He knew exactly what to do.

(To be continued, but not so fast! First, you have a whole book to get through!)

Like Red, I was making my way through the tangled yet untrodden course of young adulthood, optimistic and overconfident. Yes, I was also on a hazardous path, unaware of the danger threatening my dreams that I saw smooth and shining ahead of me. I dreamed of love and romance, meeting my perfect mate, and living the perfect life. I'd never make the mistakes my parents made. Little did I know that my Mr. Perfect was a Big Bad Wolf in disguise.

Echo And Narcissus

Once upon a time, there lived a beautiful nymph who was in service to the Olympian goddess, Hera, queen of the gods. The nymph had one grave fault. She was a notorious gossip. Having access to Hera's private life, she found much to gossip about with the other nymphs. She should have kept her lips sealed. When Hera learned of this betrayal, she was furious. As punishment, Hera allowed the nymph to speak only the last word or phrase spoken by another. Robbed of her speech and distraught, the poor nymph wandered through the forest.

One day, she came across a river and saw the most gorgeous young man kneeling at the water's edge. Instantly she was smitten. Narcissus, for that was his name, was staring into the river, where he saw a reflection of a beautiful young man seemingly gazing back at him.

"You are beautiful!" he said to his reflection.

19

"Beautiful!" repeated the nymph behind him.

"I love you!" declared Narcissus.

"Love you!" chorused the nymph longingly.

Delighted that the beautiful young man returned his feelings, Narcissus jumped into the water to join his adored one, only to drown. Finally, the gods took pity on him and turned him into a small flower found growing by the water. This flower bears his name.

The nymph faded from grief and longing and now dwells in remote areas. When you call out, you will hear an answer, but the nymph cannot speak otherwise; it is her only voice. Today we know her as Echo.

How does this relate to my experience? Certainly, an angry goddess did not punish me for gossiping. Having been raised in the Catholic Church of the 1950s, I was taught not to question but to obey. As well, my alcoholic father repeatedly silenced me. The one time I dared to talk back, to speak my truth, he could not bear to hear it, so he beat me. My true self hid in a cave inside myself, cowering and shivering, and my voice became an echo.

When Paul and I first met, it seemed that we were made for each other. He took on the role of the sun-gilded hero, and I played the pale moonlike heroine existing only to reflect and admire his golden deeds.

The third tale, *The Emperor's New Clothes,* explains how people can share the same illusion even though deep inside, they "know better," and their inner perceptions are accurate in the first place.

The Emperor's New Clothes

Once upon a time, there were two swindlers. They came across the palace of a great Emperor. They discussed how they could get gold from this ruler and decided to find his weakness. As it happened, the emperor was very vain about his appearance. He wore the finest of robes and always sought to improve his extensive wardrobe of exquisite silks, satin, brocades, and velvet. His boots were made of the finest leather.

The swindlers decided to pay a visit to this emperor. They bowed low before him, introducing themselves as tailors. "We sew the most elegant vestments in the world! The materials we use are so refined that only those who are the most intelligent and discerning can see them, whereas those who are stupid cannot see them."

The emperor was impressed. "I need new robes for a special state occasion. I shall pay you handsomely should your craft prove satisfactory."

"Oh, ever so much more than just satisfactory, Sire!" carolled the swindlers and went to work in the royal sewing room, stretching the invisible (non-existent) cloth and then hemming it with a needle and thread. Occasionally, officials would stop by to see what progress the tailors had made. Then, they would praise the swindlers' outstanding work, not wanting to appear stupid.

At last, the emperor came to see for himself. He hesitated. Was his vision deceiving him? However, remembering the remarks of his subordinates, he agreed that these clothes were of the most delicate and exquisite quality. Surely, he, the mightiest of monarchs, was the most intelligent and discerning!

"Indeed, Your Majesty. No one ever has seen their like!" For once, the deceivers spoke truly and could hardly refrain from chortling as the emperor doled out enough gold to keep them in wealth for many years to come. The following morning, they took the utmost care in dressing the emperor in

his new outfit so as not to tear that precious material. Then, as quickly as they could, the swindlers hightailed it to who knows where to enjoy their ill-gotten goods!

After the swindlers vanished, the emperor paraded proudly through the city in his new garments. The people roared their approval, afraid to offend him by pointing out the obvious. Nonetheless, a small boy cried out, "The Emperor has no clothes!" The emperor heard this but thought "nonsense," for this was only a child, and continued to strut his stuff, as vain as a peacock.

In this story, no one, including the emperor, wished others to see him as stupid, so he heaped the highest praise on the non-existent garments. Perhaps some of his subjects did the same for fear of offending their ruler. Others might have perceived the situation correctly; however, hearing the majority's opinion, they decided their perception was wrong.

In my case, I wanted something more than the truth of what was occurring. I wanted my romantic illusion that my Big Bad Wolf was the perfect man. I didn't want to hurt his feelings. I wanted peace at any price, even though it meant the cost of my sanity. I had so many inner nudges and even bodily symptoms indicating that this relationship was hazardous to my mental and physical health! Instead, I kept ignoring and suppressing my internal warning system—my BS detector.

I do not intend to blame my younger self who did not have the vision and experience that I have now. Young Elizabeth was like The Fool in the Tarot cards about to step off a cliff, blithely whistling a happy tune and gazing at a butterfly instead of looking where she was going.

Stories and myths reside in the depths of our subconscious minds. Mythmakers and storytellers draw them out into our conscious world to express truths we would rather not face. We ignore the elephant in our living room and admire the lovely paintings on our walls and the cute doilies on our furniture. If anyone points out the obvious, we say, "Elephant? What elephant?" and continue to be unaware of what is there for us to see.

3

Early Life, Early Strife

In August 1944, 21-year-old Eva joined the Warsaw Uprising as a messenger. One year later, the Germans arrested her group and transported them to Emsland, Germany. There they incarcerated the women in Oberlangen, a prisoner-of-war camp. If not for the intervention of the International Red Cross, the Germans would have sentenced the women to death. Instead, they conscripted them as slave labour for the local farmers. Conditions were grim, and the food was barely sustainable; however, they were better off than those sent to civilian concentration camps. Later the women were transferred to Bergen-Belsen, near the concentration camp.

In April 1945, the British Army liberated the women. My father, Michael, arrived with the British Army. He had been a prisoner in three POW camps, once in Germany and twice in Russia.

As soon as Dad laid eyes on pretty Eva, he was hooked. Mom told me he proposed to her three days after they met. She, of course, said, "No." Mike was not one to take "no" for an answer, though, and threatened to re-enlist in the army to fight the Japanese and possibly die. However, he had charms other than suicidal threats. Mike had a rich imagination and had entertained his buddies at the prisoner-of-war camps by making up stories in exchange for cigarettes. He would always leave his audience hanging at a crucial juncture until the following evening. His comic impersonations of officers and other characters made them howl. Plus, he was very romantic. Eva succumbed.

Three months later, there was a short, simple wedding ceremony and a celebratory dinner. Dad overdid it with the libations and got plastered. Their wedding night was a portent of things to come.

Raised in a non-drinking family, Eva had never seen anyone drunk before. Her family's idea of a good time was to turn on the radio and to read—each to their own book! She thought her new husband had gone mad. Without so much of a "good night," she ran to their room and locked the door. Where Dad slept that night, I do not know. He must have sobered up at some point and apologized; otherwise, I would not be sitting here to tell the tale!

The Polish Army moved to Dorset, England, and there in Hayden Park, my parents lived in a barracks. On September 23, 1948, I was born in the nearby town of Sherborne.

When I was small, Dad was the centre of my universe. He hoisted me up on his shoulders or pretended to be a bear chasing me. He made up stories about a clever cat and dog who outwitted a gang of thieves in a dim, dark forest. He bounced me on his knee, chanting a rhyme about a horse that started off walking slowly, then moved to a *trot, trot, trot,* and finally to GALLOP, GALLOP, GALLOP! I shrieked with laughter.

Family was everything to him. When we first arrived in our small city in British Columbia, Canada, Dad worked two jobs at the same time, painting and doing other chores. Then, thankfully, he got steady work in construction. Over time, he and Mom saved up enough to buy their own 1910 saltbox-style house. They supplemented their income by renting the two rooms on the second storey, and Mom was in charge of the tenants. Dad was very houseproud, so he puttered around our bountiful vegetable garden or watered the pristine lawn even after a long day at work. He hung a swing for me next to our wooden shed. We had the nicest yard in our block with the flower borders and all.

Our life was peaceful back then. I don't remember him and Mom quarrelling. However, as his drinking increased, he would become someone I couldn't recognize. After a few beers, his face reddened, and if he brought a buddy home with him, they started to "sing." I put the word sing in quotes because Dad couldn't carry a tune to save his life. What he lacked musically; he made up for in volume. Caterwauling would be a better way to describe it! Upon getting up, he'd sway, and his steps were uneven. Then he grew overly affectionate and pulled in whoever got in his way—usually Mom—for a sloppy kiss. As for me, I stayed out of the way, watching all of his antics with widened eyes.

This phase of Dad's behaviour wasn't too bad but the following one was scary. He would turn into the Polish version of The Incredible Hulk (a TV hero who'd turn green and monstrously muscled whenever he grew enraged). Only with Dad, his face would turn scarlet! He'd start picking on Mom, beginning with "What have you been doing all day?" then picking at her about her cleaning and cooking even though the house was tidy, and dinner was on the table. If he didn't like what she served for supper, he flung his plate of food at the kitchen wall, cursing and swearing. Then came his accusations of her alleged flirtations with other men, of flagrant unfaithfulness when he knew perfectly well, as I did, that Mom had been at home all day. He hurled ugly names at her and then the threats.

"I ought to wipe the floor with you like a rag!"

Mom shouted denials and her own accusations of his drunkenness as she grabbed his half-filled glasses and bottles of alcohol and poured them down the sink.

My room was next to the kitchen, so I heard all of these hateful exchanges in ear-splitting detail. Sometimes Mom ran in and knelt by my bed, sobbing her heart out. Was her display intended to make Dad feel guilty? Regardless, he just followed her into my room and continued yelling. Other times, I'd tiptoe into the kitchen and beg them to stop fighting. "I have school tomorrow." They lowered their voices for a few minutes, then went back to it. These arguments went on for years.

Amid all this chaos, Mom became pregnant with Alicia (Lita). Mom had told me it would be like having a living doll to play with, except dolls didn't cry all night and make my mother too tired and too busy to flutter around me as before. I'd been the center of my parents' universe for eight years. Now here was a caterwauling, pooping, eight-pound contender. As a toddler, she was so cute my neighbourhood pals wanted to play with her before proceeding on our adventures. But spoiled brat that I was, I didn't like that either.

Mom thought a second child would give Dad an incentive to stop drinking, which it did for a few months. Back then, we didn't understand the power of addiction. Dad would insist that he could control his drinking, but his subsequent periods of sobriety grew shorter and shorter. Whenever Dad did get back on the bottle, he'd blame it on something that Mom had said or done, no matter how much she tiptoed around not to offend him.

By the time my brother, Raymond, was born, I was almost a teenager and my world revolved around my peers and listening to the top forty hits on the radio. I didn't even want anyone to know I had parents, so I greeted Ray's arrival with distant benevolence. Ray was about ten and too young to be caught up in my psychodrama, but I just thought I'd give him an honourable mention!

When I was fourteen, things between Dad and myself came to a head.

It happened on a beautiful day in early June with the sun smiling down on the earth against a backdrop of the purest blue. I was dressed in a pale-blue matching outfit, a sleeveless blouse and a skirt with a pattern of tiny white flowers. My cream shoes had little kitten heels. Looking in the mirror, I felt proud and grown-up. To complete my appearance, I smoothed on pearly pink lipstick. There! I was sure to make a good impression at the Employment Office.

Berry-picking—the job I was applying for—wasn't impressive, but it sure topped babysitting, which I hated.

With a quick "bye" to Mom, I set off out of the house.

Dad was bent over, weeding along the flower border.

I waved at him.

He looked my way and then shouted, "STOP!"

I stopped.

"Wash off that lipstick at once! You look like a tramp!"

I felt bile rising within me. "NO!" I don't know why I said that. "No" wasn't a word anyone said to Dad.

Now he was standing in front of me. "You're not going anywhere until you wash it off!"

All the bitterness I'd stuffed down for years spewed out. "I HATE YOU!" I yelled. "I HATE YOU!"

"How dare you say you hate me! I work for you. I slave for you!" His hands became fists pounding on my shoulders and arms. "I send you to a private school! I pay for your piano lessons! How dare you!"

I was in shock, and I ran into the house crying. Dad had shouted at me sometimes, which was scary, but he'd never hit me. Mom had seen everything from the kitchen window. She followed me into my room, put her arms around me, and quietly held me for a few minutes as I sobbed into her shoulder.

"You'll have to apologize to him," she whispered.

"But I HATE him!" I choked out. "And he shouldn't have hit me!"

"I know," she said. "But that's the only way you'll get to go out today!"

So, yes, I washed off the damned lipstick and twisted my features into a contrite expression as I approached Dad in the yard.

"I'm sorry, Dad. I didn't mean it. I love you." The words tasted sour in my mouth. LIES!

Dad just stared at me, then turned back to flower border.

I hated, hated, hated him but I also hated Mom on that day. However, it did the trick, and I got to go berry-picking that summer.

After that incident, I learned to suppress my true feelings and only say what was pleasing to those who had power over me, a practice that made me susceptible to spiritual and emotional manipulation later in my life.

A few months after that, Mom joined Al-Anon, an organization helping families and friends of alcoholics, using the 12-step program adapted from Alcoholics Anonymous. She learned not to engage with Dad when he was drunk.

Instead, she could go for a walk or take a bath. She learned not to phone his workplace to report that he was sick when he was hungover. She did not bail him out when the police arrested him for drunk driving and crashing into a telephone pole. As a result, he spent a month in the city jail. She wasn't heartless; she visited him. As for me, I wished he'd stay in jail forever.

Things were a lot quieter in our household once Dad returned. However, he could not stay sober for long. One night, he kept haranguing Mom, even though she kept trying to walk away. Then he hit her and hit her. His blows started getting more savage. I heard the shouting and ran into the kitchen. I froze, a bowl of popcorn in my hand. My three-year-old sister ran up to Dad and struck him on the legs. She was much braver than I was. He pushed her away.

"Go!" Mom shouted at me as Dad went for her again. "Mrs. Wells!"

Mrs. Wells was an elderly widow who lived across the street from us. She watched everything in the neighbourhood and was as sharp as a tack.

I dropped the popcorn and took off. Mrs. Wells called the police. After they arrived and took Dad away in hand-cuffs, she invited Mom, Lita, Ray, and me to stay the night. Mom decided not to go back home. Fortunately, she had friends who invited us to stay with them until she could find a place of her own and get set up on welfare. I loved being away from Dad; I absolutely loved the peace and the quiet and long talks with Mom. The apartment she found was only two blocks from my school. We could hear church bells from an Episcopalian church nearby on Christmas Day. I wanted to stay there forever; however, that was not to be.

Persuaded by a Polish friend, Dad joined Alcoholics Anonymous, and after attending for a couple of months, he convinced Mom to move back in with him. She told me later she had found it too hard to stretch the welfare cheque and could not get a job after not working outside the home for years. But, even if she did, who would look after us? So back we went to live with Dad. My parents bought a larger, more modern house to make a new beginning, and they rented the second-storey apartment to a tenant.

Dad remained in AA for only a short time after our return, then again hit the bottle. Every so often, Dad would try to stop drinking without help but never succeeded. His self-imposed periods of sobriety grew increasingly shorter. Dad never went back to AA. His attendance had only been a ploy to convince Mom to return to him.

After a few years, exhausted by the wear and tear of his alcoholic descent, Mom left Dad, this time for good. As a veteran and former prisoner-of-war, she learned she was eligible for a full veteran's pension. By then, I was employed full-time as a clerk at the local library. Having dropped out of a local university, I was fortunate to get this position that enabled me to live away from home. Mom no longer needed to worry about supporting me.

Poor Dad. From that point on, his path was a downward spiral into illness, hospitalization, and eventually death. Even so, Mom was compassionate and visited him in the hospital.

As for me, I kept an icy distance apart from him, wary and mistrustful, not understanding the power of addiction until much later in my own life.

4

The God Connection

To marry my dad, Mom needed to promise the priest officiating at the ceremony to raise her children in the Roman Catholic faith. She agreed. As the eldest child, I attended an all-girl Catholic school for 12 grades. The school uniform consisted of a white shirt, navy blue tie, and a shapeless navy tunic with a belt of the same colour. We were also required to wear tams with the school insignia. In addition, there were the inevitable black oxfords that we all hated to wear. Every morning we had catechism lessons. Occasionally, the nuns would march us off to confession.

Missing mass on Sunday was an offence that was punishable by eternal damnation. I was the only one in my family who attended church on Sundays. Mom, a lukewarm Lutheran, was not sufficiently motivated, and Dad never attended in all the years I knew him. In Grade 5, when one of my classmates found out that my parents didn't go to church, she said smugly, "Your parents will go to Hell."

"That's not true!" I retorted hotly.

"Ask Sister," she told me smugly. "Sister" was our homeroom teacher.

So, I explained the situation to the nun, hoping there would be a shred of mercy shown to my delinquent parents. Instead, she nodded and told me that, yes, indeed, Mom and Dad were destined for the everlasting inferno.

I was horrified.

After school, I rushed home to tell my mom the bad news. I didn't dare bring up this subject with Dad. He'd only get angry.

"It's not true," Mom replied. "You can't take this nun too seriously. God is merciful!"

I was confused. Weren't nuns and priests closer to God than lay people? Wouldn't they know better than my mom? And Mom wasn't even a Catholic.

Oh dear, just another thing for me to worry about!

Lita and Ray did not get the benefit of a Catholic school education. By the time they started school, my parents didn't have the money to pay for tuition, uniforms, and all the other expenses.

Now here is another tale to be told. It happened in Grade 10. There were two confessional booths in the church, replete with curtains for privacy. Half the class was required to line up at one end, and the rest were to line up at the other booth. We never knew which priest we would draw. One booth concealed a kind priest, and the other contained Father Hell. At least that was what I called him. I dreaded confessing my misdeeds to Father Hell.

Did I miss a mass on Sunday? Mortal sin! Did I eat meat on Friday? Also, a mortal sin. Did I, God forbid, indulge in impure thoughts?

"DO YOU WANT TO GO TO HELL? It certainly looks like you're headed in that direction!" Even when I had committed lesser sins such as yelling at Lita and Ray or talking back to Mom, I always heard the same thing.

I'd leave that booth feeling like the scummiest of scum and the wormiest of worms, half expecting a trapdoor to open under me, and WHOOSH! I could feel the heat rising from the floor, flames licking at my oxfords.

One morning, I arrived with my class earlier than usual. We saw the two priests enter their respective booths. Immediately, we lined up for the booth with the nicer priest— yes, all forty of us!

Shortly after, Father Hell came out of his booth, intimidating in his long black cassock. Glaring at us. Tapping his foot. Arms akimbo. Our teacher motioned half of our group to line up on the other side. Reluctantly, the girls shuffled toward Father Hell's confessional. I thought he reserved his ire just for me, but I wasn't the only one. That made me feel better. Did Father Hell learn anything from this incident? No, he remained scary and unyielding. Afterwards, I figured that if I were hell-bound, at least I'd have the company of my classmates. Maybe Hell wouldn't be so bad after all!

One day, the nuns ushered us into the cathedral to attend a novena. A novena is a series of devotions honouring Mary, the mother of God, to obtain special graces.

I was kneeling on the hassock, suffering through the prayers. I was so bored I could have screamed. We'd only been there ten minutes, with at least 45 more minutes of agonized listening to the priest gabbling away in Latin. He sounded bored too.

I reverted to my favourite fantasy, which I'm embarrassed to recount. It was so hokey, but all right, if you must know, here it is.

I'm a poor but sprightly lass who learns there will be a parade in honour of a handsome young prince. However, the streets are so crowded that I can't see him. Finally, the solution presents itself as a tall tree, which I hasten to climb.

There is a large limb overhanging the parade ground—prime view!

A marching band strikes up. I watch the palace guards in their colourful uniforms marching to the beat of drums, and finally, there sits the prince in an open carriage by himself. Conveniently for me, the limb snaps, and I fall into the seat opposite his! The crowd gasps, and guards come rushing toward the carriage. Unfazed, the prince raises a hand to stop the guards and then fixes his gaze upon me. Yeah, you guessed it. My perfect, slim-waisted golden-haired gorgeousness bowls him over! The parade continues, and when it's over, my story ends with a lot of kissing.

I always stopped at this point because the church would categorize anything more than kissing as a mortal sin, and being a good Catholic girl, that's where I drew the line.

On this day, I only got as far as the tree. It felt like *something* was blocking my thoughts, as if somehow a barrier was in place. I tried to continue my fantasy but could not go forward.

So, what now? I thought of a psychology book of Mom's, which I had thumbed through about a woman who was psychoanalyzed and cured of her neurosis once she identified the trauma tormenting her psyche. Naturally, it was all her mother's fault, but I knew that it would be my dad who was to blame in my case. Aha! I'd spend the rest of the hour figuring out my major traumas.

Once again, there was the block. My thoughts could not go forward. This feeling was so strange. Was I losing my mind? What else could occupy the rest of my time here? I thought of Mom's Al-Anon pamphlet; she had just joined this group. Okay, I would go through the 12 steps. The block finally lifted.

Step One: Admitted we were powerless over alcohol—that our lives had become unmanageable. Thinking of Dad, I had no problem with that step.

Step Two: Came to believe that a power greater than ourselves could restore us to sanity. Yeah, I supposed God could if He wanted to bother.

There, two steps finished. On to Step Three. Made the decision to surrender our will and our lives over to the care of God as we understood Him. Oh no! Although I would never consciously admit it to myself, I hated God. He was easily offended and always on the lookout for my sins. His rules made it too easy to go to Hell; endless, eternal torture forever and ever. Since it would be impossible to die in a sinless state, I'd probably wind up in a dismal purgatory, waiting to be sprung by the prayers of kith and kin—if they remembered to pray for my soul. Thanks, but no thanks!

I decided to skip Step Three.

Step Four was about "taking a searching and fearless inventory of ourselves." That's what I would do.

Oh, dear! That tiresome block again. Despairingly, I stared at the clock—another half hour to go! And then—a question shaped itself in my mind in words other than my own. *"Since you are a guest in God's house, couldn't you at least let Him in on your thoughts?"*

No! I answered. But the question would not release me.

"Since you are a guest in God's house, couldn't you at least let Him in on your thoughts?"

No! said I, hoping my reply would end this weirdness. *(Go away and leave me alone!)*

Once again. *"Since you are a guest in God's house, couldn't you at least let Him in on your thoughts?"*

I heaved a sigh. *Oh, all right, God. Come on in if You have to.*

Then, no words, only a vast invisible Presence surrounding me, gazing into my soul with such love and compassion. This God knew everything about me, my thoughts and actions, past and present, good, bad, and indifferent. And it was okay because I was precious to Him.

Holy cow! Is this really happening?

This God cared about my happiness. I'd been so miserable about being unpopular at school. My classmates were not unkind; however, the plump shy girl with dandruff on her shoulder did not draw positive attention. They almost always chose me last for sports teams and spelling bees. I keenly felt the rejection. At recess and lunch hour, I attached myself to the fringes of one group or another, hoping to blend in. Beyond a polite "hi," the girls talked only to each other. I felt invisible. Eventually, I would leave, thinking there was something wrong with me. Fortunately, I always had a good novel to hide behind.

God told me, *"Whenever you see someone coming toward you in the hallway, look at them, smile, and say 'hi.'"*

I took this advice very seriously. I practiced looking up at the people I passed instead of staring at the floor. God's second suggestion was that I learn how to laugh at myself, specifically at my pratfalls, mistakes, and embarrassing moments.

I had to think a bit about developing a sense of humour; finally, I came up with the perfect idea. Every day, after lunch, a group of girls played volleyball just for fun. Anyone could join, so I did. Being slow and clumsy, I had plenty of opportunities to comment to someone nearby about my latest boo-boos. It felt weird at first. I had to steel myself and say to myself, *Okay, one, two, three— ha, ha, ha!* At first,

I had to force a laugh, but later it felt more natural. Since it wasn't a competitive game, no one minded my blunders. I extended this practice to other areas of my life as well.

Alateen was the next step for me. There, I felt the warmth and acceptance I craved from the other teens, who also dealt with a parent's alcoholism. I learned to examine my behaviour and became a nicer person to live with at home. I yelled (less) at Lita and Ray and curbed my instinct to rudely answer whenever Mom asked me to go to the grocery store or wash the dishes.

The changes I made were small but mighty. Grades 11 and 12 were my best school years. I joined the drama club, wrote for the yearbook, and hung out with a new friend. Miraculously, my baby fat melted away, and whenever I looked in the mirror, I saw a pretty girl smiling back at me.

God was my new best friend. I grew zealous about attending masses. In my bedroom, I wrapped a Japanese kimono around my nightie, lit a candle, and said a few prayers. I wrote "Dear God" letters about my daily struggles.

"Mom, I think I want to become a nun," I announced one day.

"Oh Beth, you'd be so safe, away from the cares of the world," she sniffled, wiping her eyes. Fortunately, for myself and the nuns, this phase only lasted for a couple of months.

"What?" exclaimed Mom later. "After all the tears I shed for you?" She laughed.

At the back of the church was a shelf stuffed with pamphlets: How to talk to a Protestant about Divorce; The Church's Position on Birth Control; How to explain the Church's Position on This, That, and the Other Thing. I read them all, determined to become a fierce defender of Roman Catholic morality. However, the more I read, the more I found myself on the wrong side of the argument. Coming from my chaotic home, I felt that divorce is sometimes necessary. Birth control made sense to me, thinking of my mother on welfare, unable to support her three children. These pamphlets opened a floodgate of questioning, which is likely why you don't see them anymore! As close as I felt to my Higher Power, I slowly drifted away from Catholicism.

After graduation, I held a uniform-burning ceremony. YEEHAW!

As I was considering a career in teaching, I volunteered to teach Grade One students at Sunday School. However, I felt nervous about being "in charge" and had no idea what to do with a couple of unruly kids. Besides, some of those six-year-olds were becoming too sophisticated for me.

One Sunday morning, I shared what Jesus said about God taking care of the birds, and then a little girl raised her hand.

"Teacher," she said. "I saw a cat in my yard, and he killed a bird." She looked at me, and I looked at her. What do you say to that?

"Right," I replied. "Shall we do some colouring now? I'll pass out the paper and the crayons."

Increasingly, I questioned the church's teachings and considered leaving the faith. However, confessing these doubts to Sister Mary, the nun who oversaw the Sunday school, was not the smartest thing to do.

Sister Mary broke down and wept.

Really? "Sister, why are you crying?" I asked.

"Because you're on the road to Hell," she wailed.

Oh, God! Is it a mortal sin to make a nun cry? And what if she is right? Once again, I could feel the heat rising from the floor. Would that trap door suddenly open? I cringed and remained in the church for another two years. My heart wasn't in it, though.

My friend and neighbour, Cathy, was a Baptist and very eager to share the tenets of her faith. She invited me to attend some of her church's services. I was excited that the Baptist focus was on one's personal relationship with Jesus. They passed over the various intermediaries proliferating the Catholic Church, for example, popes, cardinals, and archbishops. I enjoyed the spirited hymns they sang and the enthusiasm of the congregation. They expressed my inner truth at that time.

"Okay, Cathy, I'm in!" I told her on the way to the service. "Tonight, I'll talk to Reverend Lowry about getting baptized."

Cathy was over the moon.

However, it never happened. That evening's sermon was about the evils of the Roman Catholic Church, namely about priests selling indulgences and the heretical worship of Mary, who was NOT a member of the Old Boys' club. On and on, he ranted. Cathy looked at my face and immediately knew that she would not get a gold star for bringing in a lost sheep. She apologized to me for her pastor. She must have been feeling very sheepish.

I couldn't let that go and wrote an angry letter, the gist being that he had just lost a potential paying customer. In reply, he mailed me a pamphlet listing the evils of worshipping Mary.

Cathy and I decided to investigate other protestant churches, but none felt right for me.

Then, one night, I had an interesting dream. I dreamed I exited a cathedral, feeling very discontent and restless, and went shopping for a new coat. None of the coats I tried on fit me. That's exactly how I felt in my waking life. Thus, I ended up churchless. However, I tucked Jesus away into the church of my heart, a loving presence as I made my way into my new life as a young adult.

5

A Death in the Family

After leaving Dad for the final time, Mom put a down payment on a small house in a pleasant neighbourhood where she, Lita, and Ray settled quite happily. The question came up as to whether or not I should visit Dad. I saw a counsellor, but he was not much help. "It's up to you," he kept saying. I wavered. I knew what I wanted to do, but I wanted permission. I wanted to break free of Dad. I was fed up with so much of my family life revolving around him. I was tired of soaking up his sadness and pain.

On the other hand, I knew that Dad loved me. There was never any question of that. So, I knew that I'd feel guilty if I didn't visit him. But, oh, I didn't want that burden.

I wanted someone to say, "For your emotional health, it's better not to visit your dad." But it was up to me. In the end, I chose myself.

Maybe it would have been a lot easier for me to live with that decision if Dad hadn't come into the library from time to time. He was starting to look shabby, and he had stopped shaving. He'd shuffle up to the counter where I was working. "Beth, why don't you visit me?" It was heartbreaking to look at him. I knew that even if I did visit him, it would still be heartbreaking to see that need in his eyes. I'd murmur something about being very busy and excuse myself to the staff washroom to shed tears. I couldn't bring myself to visit him.

Two years later, before a six-month European trip, I reluctantly agreed to see him. However, I had one condition; he had to be sober during my visit. So, on the appointed day, I asked Mom, "How do I know he's sober?" It happened that Mom knew the tenant's phone number who rented the upstairs portion of the house where Dad still lived. The tenant did a quick check and phoned back to say, "No, your dad is not sober." I felt tremendously relieved. That meant I didn't have to go!

I can only imagine how nervous he was about our visit; drinking was the only way he knew how to ease his anxiety. However, I did feel some sympathy for him and sent him a postcard from London. I wrote that I loved him, although it felt fake. That was my last communication with him.

Several months later, Mom phoned long distance to my aunt (her cousin) with whom I was staying. She told me that Dad fell down the basement steps, and it was unknown if an aneurysm was the effect or the cause. In any case, his death had been instant. He had suffered more in his life than he did in his death. Even as I'm writing about his death now, my eyes are tearing up. He must have been so lonely. God bless you, Dad, wherever you are.

At that time, however, I only felt relief, blessed relief. Dad's death lifted an unbearable weight from my shoulders.

6

Date Me at Your Peril!

I wish I could say that I grew in a balanced and holistic way after my spiritual awakening, but that didn't happen. In some areas, I made excellent progress, while in others, I still had a lot of work to do. Did you ever see a kitten with oversized ears and tail? She's obviously done some growing but needs to even out, to mature into her features, and eventually does. Well, that was me.

Some of the women in my Al-Anon meeting used to say to me, "Isn't it wonderful that you discovered Al-Anon so early in your life? You won't make the same mistakes we did!" Sometimes I used to feel quite smug about that. No, I wouldn't make the same mistakes. No, I wouldn't marry an alcoholic. After all, I had the 12 steps. I was set for life.

I didn't know that I'd make my own mistakes, which would be catastrophic, unlike those of my parents, but missteps with my unique stamp. I didn't realize how much growing I had yet to do. The gross imbalance was my inability to get along with half the human race; in other words, with the male species.

Men were aliens—I knew men were from Mars long before the author wrote that book. Being thirteen when my only brother was born, and attending an all-girls Catholic school, I didn't know boys. In my limited experience, I'd learned that boys were rough and tough, loud and aggressive. They liked to wrestle. If they pitched a ball, they threw it hard, possibly hitting you. They chased you with worms, threatening to put them down your back. Or they tickled you real hard until you cried. There was even a neighbourhood bully, and he was a boy. So, no, I didn't and absolutely wouldn't play with those boys.

At school, they told me that a girl had to stay pure like the Virgin Mary. Being with a boy could lead to "occasions of sin." A girl had to be extra careful not to inflame his lust and save herself for marriage. I concluded that guys had no self-control, and I'd have to fight them off to preserve my precious virginity!

Another thing I feared was falling into the "mommy trap." To be a mother meant (to me) giving up your freedom. If you made an unhappy marriage, you either had to stay "for the kids" or struggle as a single parent.

At seventeen, I made up my mind not to have children. Later, Dad told me in a rare confidential talk that Mom had left him early in their marriage but returned when she learned she was pregnant—with me. Knowing that fact confirmed my decision: I wanted romance. I wanted to experience sex. And I did want to marry, but should the marriage not work out, I wished to escape without further complications. Later in life, watching my divorced friends struggle with work and children—especially with their teen children—confirmed my decision to remain child-free.

Just after high school, I went out with one fellow for a few months. I considered Bert to be "safe" and thought it would look good on my "dating resume" when I talked to my girlfriends. I believed it would make me appear more "normal."

Bert and I met at a school for disabled children, where we both volunteered as teaching assistants.

However, he was more of a project than a prospective boyfriend. He was the most morose person I'd ever encountered. He hated his job as an auto mechanic and was very down on himself. The few times we'd drop into the local disco, he would just sit there, glumly staring into his beer, hardly speaking, let alone getting up to dance. I decided I'd fix him and started to preach the 12 steps to him (a no-no in Al-Anon.)

Blah, blah, blah. That was me!

Bert loved it! After a few months, he confided to Mom that he wanted to marry me as I would help make him a better person.

"My daughter is not a public leaning post!" Mom retorted.

This situation had gone too far; I never did consider marrying Bert. I was preparing for university. I was rather cool to the poor guy. He never received so much as a single kiss.

Dad had a good grasp of the situation. He took me aside and said, "If you don't care for Bert, break off with him. It's not nice to lead him on."

Reluctantly, I conceded that Dad (for once) was right. and I parted ways with Bert.

When I was nineteen, my friend Rosie and I joined the Catholic Youth Organization. This church-sponsored group was for young Catholic singles to meet and hopefully marry other young Catholic singles.

The CYO organized car rallies, beach picnics, dances, and singing on a float for the Victoria Day Parade, but I was too nervous to enjoy them. I didn't know how to joke, laugh, and flirt with boys like the other girls. I could hardly carry on a regular conversation. One of the girls told me years later that I'd stare at the floor whenever a fellow started talking to me. I was a deer caught in the headlights, even though they were regular guys and not that scary. I was pretty enough to draw attention, but I didn't consider these guys to be "safe," so I only went out on group outings.

Eventually, the organization dissolved when most members paired up and left for matrimonial bliss, as did the young priest who had supervised us and left the priesthood a few years later; but that's another story! Now I was left on my own in the big, bad dating world.

My experience with Rob finally convinced me that I should get some help. I lived in an old Victorian mansion converted into a boarding house. Rob was a neighbour, a cute, nice guy around my age. We'd walk together to our respective jobs—parting ways at the library, and from there, he continued to the small firm where he worked as a drafts-man. We became friendly and would occasionally visit a coffee shop nearby. Since these were not actual dates, I felt safe.

One of his complaints was that his dad had told him to "never marry a virgin," but he always developed feelings for chaste girls. He managed to coax me to kiss him on the cheek on his birthday, but it took a lot of doing on his part. Then he started preaching at me about how virginity was outdated. He was harmless, but I began to feel insecure around him.

I agreed when he asked me to go out with him on New Year's Eve. We would spend the evening at this cool bar with live music. I intended to go but I panicked about what would happen at midnight. So silly! After all, if I didn't want to kiss him, I didn't have to. On the appointed evening, however, I flew the coop with nary a word to Rob and stayed overnight at Mom's instead.

As I slunk back to my room the next morning, another tenant accosted me, telling me how devastated Rob was and how he'd cried most of the night. So off to Rob's room I went, apologizing profusely. I meant it, too. I hated that I'd caused so much pain. However, it was a one-off, right? I'd do better next time, wouldn't I? Nope!

In April, when I was 21, I had saved enough money to visit my aunt in London, England, and go to Poland to meet my relatives. Maybe later, I could take a tour to see Paris! While Mom helped me carry my suitcases to her car, Rob asked me to pop over to his room to say "goodbye" and give him my address in London so we could write to each other. I agreed. But guess what? I ditched him again!

I tried not to care that I'd twice broken his heart. However, the episode burned itself into my mind and caused me to finally reach out for help when I returned from my European adventure.

7

A Place of My Own

In October, upon my return, I settled temporarily with Mom while I was taking a six-month office course that featured typing, Pittman shorthand, grammar, and all the practical things I'd need to know to make a living. Later, I was fortunate to find work as a clerk-stenographer for the BC Government in a personnel department. Mr. Phillips liked that I was volunteering for the Crisis Line and thought I'd have a nice touch with people coming up to the counter to apply for work. I liked him, got along with his senior secretary, enjoyed my new job, and used my shorthand.

It was now time for me to move out on my own. The boarding house had been a trial run.

My new digs were close to the downtown area, in a small, nondescript three-storey building that reminded me of a genteel aging woman. If her clothing was a little shabby, it was clean and sported patches in the worn spots. A respectable couple managed it, made sure to keep up with the cleaning and repairs, and rented the furnished bachelor and one-bedroom apartments. While it's true that the furniture didn't always match, it was sturdy enough.

My friend Rosie claimed the bigger of the two available apartments with a tiny bedroom.

I didn't mind. There seemed to be something special about the tiny alcove in my small space. It was big enough to contain a little closet, a chest of drawers, and a single bed. Only a curtain separated it from the main living area. I spent many a cozy winter evening in bed, reading and listening to the radio, and with my phone beside me, I didn't even have to get up to make phone calls to my friends.

The main room contained a chesterfield across from the window. Behind the couch was a small kitchen table with two chairs, and behind that area a kitchenette with a small window over the sink. I had no TV, but I could always pop over to Rosie's to watch the latest shows.

Rosie was an ideal neighbour, never intrusive and always pleasant. She and I knew each other from school. Sometimes we'd go out to catch a movie or attend a CYO meeting. Aside from my dating problems, this period was one of the happiest of my life.

I'd come back home from work and survey my small domain. There was the couch with a gaily patterned orange and red Indian bedspread I'd thrown over it. Next to it was my all-important fifteen-dollar guitar. (I'll tell you the significance in a minute.) On the wall above the table—covered in a cheery orange vinyl tablecloth—I hung up a poster that portrayed the silhouette of a girl in profile sitting on a large rocky overhang. Varying shades of red filled the evening sky, and a yellow sun dipped into the horizon. On the lower right-hand corner of the poster were these words:

I believe in the sun even when it is not shining
I believe in Love even when I am alone
I believe in God even when He is silent

On top of a small bookcase, close by, was my record player. Every night after supper, I danced to Cat Steven's *Tea for the Tillerman* album. Cat's music spoke to me. His songs were about me, my hopes, and my ambitions.

> *Well, I left my happy home*
> *to see what I could find out*
> *I left my folks and friends with the*
> *aim to clear my mind out*
> *Well, I hit the rowdy road*
> *and many kinds I met there,*
> *many stories told me of*
> *the way to get there—oooh*
> *So, on and on I go,*
> *the seconds tick the time out,*
> *there's so much left to know,*
> *and I'm on the road to find out.*

As much as I enjoyed my job, I considered it a mere steppingstone for when I would be a singer-songwriter just like Cat. That fifteen-dollar guitar propelled me from writing long-winded poems as a teen to composing songs.

With the twin burdens of my alcoholic father and the Catholic Church lifted from my shoulders, my spirit soared as it never had before.

Songs flowed through me—whole and complete—with music and lyrics. Was it I who wrote them? I had to keep a notebook and pen handy at all times, as I never knew when one would conk me on the head like a ripe, juicy apple falling from a tree. The songs were in a folksy style, folk music, the genre of that time. Here's one.

Child in the Midst of Wonder

Are we just leaves to fall from a tree?
Are we just wings no more to flutter?
Are we the last notes of winter harmony?
Raindrops rolling down a gutter
Raindrops rolling down a gutter

Are we an accident that happened just by chance,
chemical by-products of the night,
pawns of the evolutionary dance?
I wish to God that I could see the light
Wish to God that I could see the light

I am a lonesome wanderer, I like to seek and ponder,
and every day grow fonder of all I see out yonder
I see love, love, the miracle love, a child in the midst of wonder
I see love, love, the miracle love, a child in the midst of wonder

If I asked the birds a-singing on that tree
If I asked the flowers that surround me
If I could ask that stream as it rushes past by me
I wonder what their answer then would be
wonder what their answer then would be

The universe is mine, material and divine
And everything's in line with
the soul strings of my mind
I see love, love, the miracle love,
a child in the midst of wonder
I see love, love, the miracle love,
a child in the midst of wonder

Yes, that's who I was back then—a child in the midst of wonder. One woman described me as "bubbly," and that's how I felt; effervescent, like champagne bubbling up after the cork has been removed from the bottle, bursting out of its glass prison.

8

All This and a Shaman Too!

S nug as a bug in a rug in my beloved small apartment on one wet and windy fall day, I decided to write down a list of qualities I wanted to see in my ideal man.

Spiritual had to be the top priority. If he didn't have a relationship with God, I wasn't interested. He didn't have to be a traditional Christian since I no longer was, but he had to believe in something greater than himself in order to understand me. So, I wrote down *spiritual* as well as,

artistic
creative
intelligent
open-minded
a professional
romantic
nice-looking

Maybe my list was the cause of all the trouble. According to positive thinking, if you write down and affirm your desires, the universe, your humble servant, shall bring them raining down upon you. However, we humans don't always think of everything. For example, the man who showed up seemed to have all the qualities on my list, BUT. . .

It all began with a phone call to Mom.

Now a widow, Mom had to act as both mother and father to my fourteen-year-old sister and eleven-year-old brother. Lita was a rebel to the core. She and Mom had regular screaming matches. Lita would sneak out of the house, go to God-knows-where, and lie to Mom about her whereabouts. (Lita told us some years later that she attended wild parties given by two young guys in their twenties who lived a few blocks away. Maybe it's just as well that Mom didn't know that at the time!)

Lita hated rules and curfews so much that she often threatened to go to child protection services to get into a foster home. Occasionally, when visiting, I found the melodrama funny, with Mom yelling, "NO!" while blocking the front door to prevent Lita's escape. Then, one day, Mom got wise. "Okay," she said. "You want to go to a foster home? How about I pack a suitcase for you? But before I do, consider this. Here you have a home where you are loved, and my rules aren't all that strict. At a foster home, they don't love you. They might have an even stricter curfew and expect you to do more chores. But if you want to leave, go ahead."

Lita let out a great groan, obviously deflated. She and Mom still had their rows, but Lita never used that threat again.

That day on the phone, Mom gave me an update on Lita. The police had picked her up with a few of her underage friends for drinking beer and looking at pornographic magazines in an abandoned ruin of an old house. The boys had burned holes in the strategic places of the nude models. Then, Mom knew it was time to admit she was powerless over Lita and needed extra help—her neighbour recommended Paul from Social Services.

Then I told Mom my sad tale of dating failures. "I know I need help, but I can't go for counselling during the day! I don't want my boss to know I have problems."

"Oh, Beth!" Mom exclaimed. "What about Paul? He is so spiritual and compassionate. You could talk to him about anything. He also works evenings, so you could see him then!"

I liked the sound of that, so the next day, I made an appointment with Paul. Yes, he would see me in the evening, but it would have to be at my home as his office was closed then.

On that fateful Tuesday evening, I opened the door to a tall, nice-looking older man with white hair. He resembled the movie actor Tom Hanks in that his face was one you felt you could instantly trust. He was dressed conservatively in a gray suit and striped shirt. After motioning him to my minute kitchen table, I made us some tea. I studied the tablecloth, wishing I'd never made an appointment with this total stranger.

"Let me tell you a bit about myself," he began, "so that you know where I'm coming from." And so, he did. He was 57 years old, married for 35 years, with two kids and many foster kids. He and his wife, Louise, had what he described as a beautiful marriage. During World War Two, he'd gone to fight overseas in Europe, was wounded, and honourably discharged.

After the war, he was able to attend a university, where he discovered his true vocation as a social worker. The Canadian government paid for his higher education as a returning veteran.

"I see it as my mission to help as many people as possible," he told me. "And that's why I work the extra hours. I'm here to serve God. Of myself, I'm nothing; I am only God's tool to use as He wills."

My eyes widened at this mention of God, although I did flinch a bit at his use of "God's tool." Then, shyly, I pointed out the poster hanging on the wall across from us.

From his reaction, I knew I could share my spiritual experience.

"You know, back when I was fifteen, I had a spiritual experience. It took place during a mass at church. I wasn't looking for it. In fact, I resisted it at first. This thought kept coming up (not my own) saying, 'since you are a guest in God's house, couldn't you at least let Him in on your thoughts?' I said 'no' the first couple of times, but the third time I gave in. All at once, I felt the most beautiful and loving Presence all around me. God knew everything about me, all my thoughts and actions—good and bad and loved me just the way I was."

"Wow!" said Paul when I finished. "That's so beautiful. That's how God is—loving, accepting, and forgiving."

Before I knew it, our time was up. After Paul left, I sat there in a daze. Was this man for real? He seemed to understand me. I could hardly wait to see him the following week.

The next Tuesday, Paul was again sitting across from me at the table.

"I'd like to talk about my dad," I began.

"You haven't mentioned him at all yet." Paul looked at me encouragingly.

"He was an alcoholic and he was always picking fights with my mom. He'd yell at her and call her ugly names. She'd cry, shout back at him, and pour his whisky and beer down the sink. This commotion would go on all night even though I had to go to school the next morning. I'd ask them to stop, but they'd just carry on. After years of this craziness, I hated my dad."

"It must have been very difficult for you."

"It was. And it got worse. Dad started to hit her. Mom left him for about six months, with the three of us kids in tow, but she found it hard to make the welfare money stretch. So, when he promised to go to AA, we went back to him. I didn't want us to go back. It was so nice and peaceful just being with Mom."

"I can see why you felt that way," said Paul. "What happened then?"

"Dad quit AA and started drinking once more. Even though he never raised a hand to her again, their relationship deteriorated, so a few years later, Mom left him for good. At that time, I was nineteen and living on my own."

"And how did that feel?"

"I felt relieved—at first—until I got a phone call from a counsellor who told me I had the choice to visit Dad or not. Now here's the thing. I knew Dad loved me and wanted me to visit him, but I didn't want to. So, I went to see this counsellor. I wanted him to tell me not to see Dad for the sake of my mental health. But, instead, he kept repeating that it was up to me."

"What did you decide?"

I sighed. "I decided not to; I felt tired of the turmoil and the pain he caused. I didn't want to deal with him anymore. I just wanted to break free and live my own life. Only, he'd come around to the library where I worked, up to the counter.

He'd look at me with tears in his eyes and say, "Beth, why don't you visit me?" It was awful! I'd just tell him I was too busy. Then I'd run into the staff washroom and cry, though I didn't change my mind about not seeing him."

I wiped a few tears from my eyes. "I feel so guilty. Al-Anon says that alcoholism is a sickness like cancer, and we're supposed to be understanding, but I didn't care. I just didn't want to deal with him—period! And then, a couple of years later, while I was in London staying with an aunt, I got a long-distance phone call. Dad died from an aneurism. The upstairs tenant found him. Dad must have felt so lonely. I feel so bad for hurting him."

"You were caught between a rock and a hard place," answered Paul. "That was one heck of a tough decision! Your choice not to visit your dad is very understandable. You wanted to protect yourself after all the years of being torn apart emotionally."

I nodded. That's how it was.

My next topic concerned my deep unease with men.

"I've never gotten along with men. I don't trust them. When I go out on a date, I'm a nervous wreck. I don't want them to hit on me, but they seem to want too much too soon. Though at times, I've hurt some nice guys who didn't deserve it. Like Rob, my neighbour in the boarding house where I lived."

I filled Paul in on how I ditched Rob on New Year's Eve and then a second time just before I left for Europe. It's true Rob said that his dad told him never to marry a virgin, but really, he was all just talk. I could have at least said "goodbye" to him. Instead, I broke his heart again.

"I feel like such a bitch! How will I ever get into a long-term relationship if I keep behaving like this? I'd like to get married someday. What's wrong with me?"

Paul shook his head. "There's nothing wrong with you. These boys you tell me about sound immature and out after only one thing. You, on the other hand, have high principles. Someday, you'll meet a young man who is truly worthy of you, who truly appreciates the lovely young woman that you are."

Huh? I stared at him. I felt deflated. These words were very nice to hear, and sometimes it was what I told myself to excuse my anti-social behaviour; however, it didn't feel right. *How is this rationalization supposed to help me get along with the opposite sex? I know I have a problem and I want to know what to do about it.*

That evening I learned even more about Paul. He was psychic! He'd given messages to friends and families during the war worrying about their "boys." And get this! Years later, he made friends with an Indigenous medicine man who taught him shamanic skills. Paul painted, too, in oils—landscapes and seascapes! What couldn't this man do?

When he left, I felt sad. This man got me, understanding me on a deeper spiritual level that was lacking in the young guys I'd previously met. He saw who I was inside. He had an abiding relationship with God, as did I. And he was so compassionate and understanding. I'd probably never meet anyone like him again. The following week would be my last session with him, and I had already told him everything that was weighing me down. What would I talk about? Moreover, there was a further complication. I'd fallen in love with him.

Paul was married—a beautiful marriage, he'd said. I had to let him go. So, all that week, I wailed along with Mary Magdalene on my Jesus Christ Superstar LP; *I don't know how to love him, what to do, how to move him.*

But enough of the wailing. I'd write a special song for him, then sing it for him, and give him the lyrics, something he could remember me by.

However, I'd keep my feelings to myself because I knew from my reading what he'd say. He would talk to me about "transference" and how many clients imagine themselves to be in love with their counsellors. He'd say he was flattered, but it would be inappropriate for him to respond, advising me to save it for someone more suitable. And I'd feel humiliated, utterly humiliated! So next week, it was to be "goodbye."

I got mad at God. "How dare You dangle a man like that in front of me? A man I can never have? I'll never meet anyone like him again! Is this some cruel joke?"

9

Love Declared

During our next appointment, sitting across the table from Paul, I kept faltering in my speech and looking away, making a lot of small talk. Work was going fine. My boss gave me an excellent appraisal. Mom and I were very close. Besides thinking Lita was a spoiled, obnoxious brat, I got along reasonably well with her. I had my songs, books, friends, and volunteer work on the Crisis Line. Life was good. I'd been struggling to find some things to talk about with him, only I didn't have anything else to confide.

"I can sense a barrier between us," said Paul after a while. "Is there something you're finding difficult to tell me?"

"Um. Well, I've been feeling sad, this being our last session."

"Yes?" prompted Paul.

Have you ever seen a tomato blush? I stared at my hands; my plain, short nails slightly chewed at the edges—a bad habit.

"What is it?" asked Paul.

"Well—I've fallen in love with you," I blurted out, wishing I was sitting under, not at, the table. "And I wrote a special song for you."

"Why, that's wonderful!" exclaimed Paul. "I fell in love with you the first time we met, but I never dreamed you would return my feelings. And I am also feeling sad because there won't be a reason to come back to see you again after tonight."

Wasn't he supposed to make the "transference" speech?

"Would you play your song for me? I'd love to hear it."

I passed him the paper with the words. "This is for you to keep, to remember me by," I said huskily. "It's a love song from God." I picked up my guitar.

God Song

All of my rivers, all of my streams
flow past my vision in parade of my dreams
All of my children, the happy, the sad
when will they learn there's no good, no bad
Do they know, will they know, who I am, what I am
I am love
They hide in my shadow, blind to their pain,
deaf to my silence that calls them by name.

They follow the rivers or play by the shore
scattering flowers, they plunge into war
seek their reflections in the mud and the slime
caught in the web and the prison of time
Do they know, will they know,
who they are, what they are
They are Love.
They hide in my shadow, blind to their pain,
deaf to my silence that calls them by name.

When will they listen to the song of my heart
how soon discover we are never apart
Do they know I love them, these poor children of mine
When will they, when will they learn, we are one
Will they find who we are, what we are
do they know, will they know
All is love, all is love, is love.

Paul had tears in his eyes. "I'm very honoured. You have a beautiful, warm voice, and the words are incredible." There was a silence. Then he said musingly, "But how can this be? How could we possibly have a relationship?"

I sat there goggle-eyed. Here I was saying "goodbye," and he was actually contemplating a relationship with me! Could this be happening?

He continued. "We can think about this over the coming week and talk about it next Tuesday."

Well, after Paul left, I was torn between disbelief, embarrassment, and jubilation. I sure did some serious praying that week. *God, if this isn't supposed to happen, please prevent it; only I DO want it to happen. But it's wrong! I'm not supposed to be thinking of him in this way. Please God, do something!*

But God must have been looking in another direction.

The following week, Paul told me even more about himself. "You should know more about who I am before making up your mind," and he invited me to ask questions.

"You said you have a beautiful marriage; isn't this going to hurt Louise?"

"Our marriage hasn't been sexual for years," he replied. "Louise and I married when we were quite young. We've grown apart in many ways. However, she's a wonderful woman. We have our children, and, over the years, we dedicated ourselves to our foster kids as well. However, I want you to know that I'll never divorce her."

"Of course not!" I exclaimed. "I don't want to be a homewrecker."

"Louise is in love with someone else," he said, watching my reaction. "Once a year, she goes away for a week or two. I know she goes to meet him."

This news boggled my mind. "And you accept this?"

He did, but I was confused. How was that a "beautiful marriage"?

I don't want to break up his home and family, but if I could be with him for a little while, even if only a few times, I'll carry away a beautiful memory and he'll always remember me. Then we can continue with our individual lives.

Paul also told me he had suffered from two "nervous breakdowns" and was hospitalized both times. He didn't mention his diagnosis and I didn't want to tread on a sensitive area.

"Did you like your psychiatrist?"

"Him? No, he's a cold-blooded bastard! Hardly human."

Oops! Painful subject. I must admit that as he talked, the play of light and shadow emphasized the lines on his face. I felt a faint stirring of doubt. He was older, so much older than me.

"Well, I've told you everything I can about myself," he said at length. "But you should know I can no longer be your counsellor."

I was very impressed by his honesty. This man had opened himself up to me completely, exposing his vulnerability. After all, he didn't have to tell me about his breakdowns!

Shyly, I said, "Yes, I do want to be with you, even if only for a short time."

It was then that we kissed. As we did, Paul whispered, "Helen."

I pulled away.

He looked embarrassed. "Helen is my ideal woman. My fantasy. You are Helen come to life."

"Oh." I smiled up at him. *But can I possibly live up to being your dream woman?*

WOW! I can hardly believe this! Next week we'll come together—as lovers!

I was so excited that I could hardly breathe. It was all I could do to focus on my work. During my lunch break, I saw my doctor about birth control. In the meantime, Paul could use condoms. Oh my God, I could hardly believe it! Was it me doing these things?

On Saturday, I went barrelling down to Misty's, a posh shop specializing in lingerie. What to buy? I felt too shy to get the tarty, see-through garment, but I didn't want to look too virginal. After some searching, I found a lovely long sleeveless gown—empire-style in pale green silk with a deep V-neck. It had silken embroidery in blue, yellow, and pink around the neck and just under the bust area.

The sales lady caught my exuberance. "Are you getting married?" she asked.

I blushed. "No." Let her wonder.

Next, it was off to the Bay to buy floral sheets and pillowcases. After all, I had to decorate my bower as well! Finally, at the bookstore, I purchased *The Sensuous Woman* by "J," which was all the rage that year, for some pointers. Honest to goodness, some of the stuff in that book! I put it in the trash twice but then fished it out to read some more. No wonder "J" didn't want to print her real name!

Now, how to go about this epic occasion?

I felt too shy to greet Paul in my nightie, but I had it laid out on my bed. I'd pulled back the bed covers to reveal the new sheets and pillowcases in all their glory. The lamp on my small dresser cast a cozy glow in my boudoir.

I always told Rosie ahead of time about the counsellor coming to see me, and she'd respected my request not to disturb us, so I felt secure that we would have no intrusion.

At last! The knock! Paul stood at the threshold, shifting his weight from one foot to the other. He seemed relieved when I made the usual offer of a cup of tea. Maybe I should have bought wine or champagne, only I didn't think of it, and apparently neither did he. We sat at the table.

Paul asked if I had changed my mind.

I looked at him sharply. *Who me? After all the trouble I'd gone to?* I shook my head "no." Then, I asked, "Have you?"

Paul sighed deeply. "No, I've been living for this moment all week, but I have to admit I'm feeling nervous."

"Me too," I said.

We both studied the floor.

I thought he'd take the initiative, being married and all, but he just sat there. Finally, I rose from the table. "I'll—um—go and change." Trembling, I disappeared behind the curtain into my alcove and quickly changed into my gown.

When I reappeared, his delighted expression spoke volumes. He followed me into the alcove, and things proceeded very naturally. What I liked the best, however, was the wonderful feeling of closeness afterwards—the afterglow!

10

Gifts

One evening, Paul told me that he wanted to buy a gift for me— "Anything you want, darling."

I knew just the thing.

For some time, I'd been passing by Tang's Pagoda and pressing against the window to look longingly at the Japanese Geisha dolls. They were about 18 inches high and dressed in the most beautiful kimonos in brightly coloured silks, satin, and brocades. The sashes were in contrasting materials and designs. Jewelled combs and silk flowers adorned the dolls' hair.

"Is there a budget?" I asked.

"No, just tell me what you want, and I'll buy it for you."

I told Paul about the dolls, giving a full description. "They're in the window at Tang's. You can't miss them!"

Paul laughed. "Anything to make you happy."

I decided then and there to buy Paul something special also. It would be a surprise. So, on the following Saturday, I stopped at Tang's. They had some beautiful men's robes, and I found the perfect one—a rich midnight blue silk with oriental symbols and a dark blue lining that would bring out his blue eyes. It cost $40, which in 1971 was a considerable sum for me.

Before Paul arrived the next week, I cleared a special corner for my new doll. I pictured her adding elegance and grace to my rag-tag apartment. I'd have to research Japanese names, for, of course I had to give her a name. I felt like a little girl waiting for Santa Claus.

I flew to the door to embrace Paul. "I didn't tell you, but I have something special for you too," I told him as he took his seat. I drew out the large gift box.

"You didn't have to do that!"

"Go on, open it!"

Paul fingered the rich silken folds. "It's beautiful!"

"Try it on."

It looked wonderful on him. "I love it, darling!" he enthused.

I was so pleased by his reaction. At the time, I never questioned where he would wear it. He'd take it home, and then what? How would he explain it to Louise? Would he wind up keeping it in its box in a closet?

"Well, now, I have your special gift," said Paul, smiling.

I felt puzzled as he drew out two small packages from his coat pocket.

"Open them, darling!" he urged.

When I did, I couldn't believe what I saw. I looked up at Paul to see if he was joking, but his expression was serious. The doll was a Chinese baby doll, four inches high, wearing a blue cotton jacket and straw hat. She didn't even have legs but stood on a wooden base. When I pulled the small plastic tree out of the other box, I figured out that she was to stand under it.

"This *is* what you wanted, isn't it, Beth?"

A lump formed in my throat. Dumbly I nodded.

"I just knew that was it! I looked at those Geisha dolls, and they were so cold and stiff and hard looking. So, I thought that couldn't possibly be what you want. You're so warm and loving and nurturing, so I went inside and got this one for you instead. You do like it, don't you, darling?"

"Of course," I choked out. I wanted to cry. Were the dolls I admired so cold-looking? Did wanting one make me a cold, heartless person? What had he paid for this baby doll and her tree? Three, four dollars? I'd have understood if he'd told me he was short of money. I'd asked him, didn't I? It wasn't about the money, but he said anything I wanted. He had promised.

After Paul left, I resentfully placed the baby doll and tree in the special space I'd created in the corner, though what I felt like doing was to throw them away.

A few weeks later, Paul told me he was making "something special" for me.

The "something special" was a native necklace with the most intricate beadwork. He hadn't finished it yet but decided to tell me about it. He said the symbols on it were against a dark blue background.

"If you had been a virgin, they would be on a white background," he told me.

I stared at him. "But Paul! Until I met you, I was a virgin."

"Oh." He sounded surprised.

Had he not been listening to me?

"I did tell you that I was frightened of men and wouldn't let anyone near me."

"Oh, I thought maybe—" he fumbled for words.

I couldn't believe his misunderstanding. What a pity that I had already laundered the evidence. I'm sure that a Medieval mother-in-law would have been delighted to see that I had been a good girl!

"Well, in that case, I'll start a new one for you."

"No, don't bother," I demurred. "You've already gone to some trouble with it."

"I know. I'll give the blue one to your sister."

"But Lita is your client, and as far as I know, she's still a virgin. So, isn't it rather strange for you to make a gift for her?"

"No, not at all," Paul said blandly. "I plan to give small gifts to your mother and brother too."

I wasn't so sure about how appropriate gift-giving was for a counsellor.

The necklace he made for me was truly gorgeous. The beads in the background were a translucent white. The symbols in orange-red, dark green, and yellow stood out. The arrows stood for truth, the orange red flowers for love, and the bottom part displayed the thunderbird, the highest form of protection.

"I'll always treasure it," I told him.

11

The Letter

One night, after Paul left, I wrote him this letter.

Dearest Paul,

I like to think of us as two rivers that meet at an intersection. For a time, their waters intermingle and flow as one but inevitably must part. I don't know how long we'll be together; however, I'll always carry a part of you wherever I go as you will always carry a part of me. In this way, we can always be together. Whatever may happen in the future, I will always love and remember you.

Beth

This letter was my way of letting Paul know that I didn't want to complicate his life or his marriage and that when it came time to let go, I was willing to do that. I, too, had a path to follow and dreams to fulfill.

When he read the letter, he choked up and said it was beautiful.

I wish I had been faithful to my sentiments in that letter. It was an honest communication of how I felt. I believe my letter was a turning point that intensified the dysfunctional nature of our relationship. Paul now knew that I saw ours as a brief but beautiful romance. On his part, he did not wish to let me go. He wanted a lifetime commitment.

12

A Wedding and
Two Curses

Just after the new year, Paul said he had something to ask me—if I wished to enter into a spiritual marriage with him. *What is that?* I wondered. I'd never heard of such a thing.

"It wouldn't be legally binding," he hastened to explain, "but it would draw us even closer together. It's okay if you say 'no,' but I just thought I'd ask."

"If it's not legally binding, what kind of ceremony would there be?" I asked curiously.

"It would be a native ceremony," he said. "Take some time to think about it."

So, I did some thinking. The term "spiritual marriage" had a permanent ring to it. I didn't want our relationship set in stone. He would still stay married to Louise; I knew that. But, on the other hand, I was in love and wanted to please him. It all sounded so romantic, and Paul told me it wasn't legally binding. What a lovely memory to have when I was an old lady. So, when he phoned back, I told him I wanted to go through with it.

"Darling!" He greeted me jubilantly the following Tuesday when he arrived and gave me a big hug. "This is going to be so wonderful. Now I know we are truly soul mates. Do you know what a soul mate is?"

"I've read something about it," I answered vaguely.

"When God first created human beings, he created man and woman together fused as a single soul, but they split apart as they came to earth. Now each seeks out their other half, for until you find your soul mate, you are never truly happy or complete."

"Would you explain this ceremony in more detail?" I asked.

"It was taught to me by a shaman. He passed on a few years ago, but now he is one of my guides. I would have to prepare myself for our marriage by fasting for three days before it."

"And what would I do to prepare for this?"

"Nothing, darling, but during the three days of my fast, my guide, this shaman, will watch you and see if you are worthy of being my mate."

"Hmm." The idea of some ghostly shaman spying on me didn't exactly enthrall me.

"For the ceremony itself, you need to have two things ready—some bread and a glass of water. First, I will drink the water and then share it with you. Then I will chew the bread and share that with you. But the most important part is with the knife."

"Knife?"

"In the native tradition, the hunting knife represents the man's soul. In the marriage, he gives it over to the keeping of his wife, who becomes the keeper of his soul. Isn't that beautiful?"

Yow! This ceremony sounds like heavy stuff. Do I want to be the keeper of a man's soul? Isn't that up to God?

Paul noticed my startled expression. "It's a great honour, darling. Soul mates can always trust one another. What happens is that I'd give you my hunting knife, and you'd keep it for me."

I nodded, still uneasy.

"Then we'd say our vows, and that would be it."

"What are the vows?"

"Mine would be 'if I ever leave this woman, may I be killed by the knife!'"

What?

"Oh, don't worry, darling," he said quickly, hearing me gasp, "that would never happen."

"Would I have to promise that too?"

"No, no! The woman says, 'if I ever leave you, may I be unhappy for the rest of my life.' After that, I'll give you a new name, a native name."

This whole thing sounds scary. I'm not sure about this. I didn't raise my doubts with Paul. Instead, we set a date.

Paul managed to wrangle a Saturday afternoon off for our ceremony.

I'd passed the previous three days looking over my shoulder. Did the ghostly shaman follow me around the whole time, or did he pop in intermittently? Was he peeking over my shoulder as I typed letters at the office? Did he watch me peel potatoes and cut up carrots for my supper? Did he run a skeletal finger along the window ledge to see if I'd dusted properly? Did he listen as I worked on my songs? One thing I'll tell you, my usual long soaks in the tub were out of the question! In any case, whatever kind of test it was, I passed. Paul was pleased to inform me that I had been found "worthy."

Then came the day. The January sun was barely managing to break through the clouds. Going into the woods was out of the question on this snowy, blowy day, so the ceremony was to take place in my humble abode. Luckily, Rosie was away for the weekend.

I wore a simple skirt and a dark green top. Around my neck hung the necklace Paul made for me. The bread and water were on my coffee table. Paul arrived wearing a burgundy shirt with casual gray slacks.

The ceremony; how would I describe it? I hate to say it, but mostly it felt hokey. Maybe if it took place in a more natural setting, it would have felt more spiritual.

For some weird reason, I thought about my best friend, Angel. Since she married and moved out of town, I hadn't seen much of her, but I felt her spirit hovering, waiting to launch into a giggling fit. We were both very good at that. First, the nuns almost tossed us out during a bishop's funeral when we got in line to kiss the bishop's ring, because it was hard for us not to laugh. Then, a dog wandered into the cathedral, which really set us off.

I tried not to picture her face as Paul and I knelt before the coffee table. He lifted the glass and drank but didn't swallow the water. Instead, he wrapped an arm around my back and dipped me as if we were doing the tango. Then, he pressed his mouth to mine to "share" the water with me.

I mustn't choke. Mustn't laugh, or I'll lose it for sure.

Then it was the same thing with the bread. Paul chewed and I got dipped once again. GROSS! I had to force myself not to spit out the remains of the bread. I wanted to retch. Somehow, I managed not to. I felt a giggle coming on. *Go away, Angel!* And she did just when I needed her the most. We now reached the scary part of the ceremony.

Paul produced this long hunting knife encased in a leather sheath. "I, Gray Wolf, give my soul into the keeping of this woman, my wife, Fawn," he intoned.

Fawn? A cute little helpless fawn? I was a young woman about to pursue her dreams and ambitions, full of hope and bright excitement. I felt like a rocket ready to launch, explore, discover strange new worlds, and seek out new civilizations. *Okay, okay, so shoot me, I'm a Trekkie. I've got to stop this nonsense, but "Fawn" is not who I am. Well, too late now.*

He handed me the knife. I stared as if it was a live snake writhing in my hand. *I don't want it! I don't want to be responsible for his soul. This part is too much. What have I got myself into?*

"God, if I ever leave this woman, may I be struck dead by the knife!"

He can't possibly be serious! It must be just his way of expressing his love for me. Gripping the knife in my hand, I decided to throw caution to the wind. "And may the knife also kill me should I ever leave this man!" I intoned.

Paul's jaw dropped. "Darling, you should never have said that! It's dangerous!"

Of course, I added the agreed-upon "may I be unhappy for the rest of my life." What a good little fawn I was!

After the ceremony, he was positively ecstatic, almost dancing on air. He told me this was the happiest day of his life. He kissed me exuberantly. The more buoyant Paul was, the more weighed down I felt. There was a bad feeling in my stomach as if I'd eaten something indigestible. My saliva tasted bitter—like bile.

When Paul left, he practically skipped out the door. Listlessly, I put the knife into its new hiding place, in the suitcase under my bed; I drank some water and popped a Gravol and an aspirin for my raging headache.

Thank God that's over!

But my subconscious mind stored the whole thing for future reference, and someday, there would be hell to pay.

And there was.

13

Psychic Experiments

Paul said he could look into the future, so naturally, I wondered about mine. His face lit up. "You have a wonderful destiny, darling. Your destiny is to become a social worker and continue my work."

"Hmm."

His eyes shone. "The best part is that I'll always be with you even after I die. I'll become your guide, advising and encouraging you for the rest of your life. Beautiful to imagine, isn't it, darling?"

"Oh, yes, Paul, it is."

But deep down, I was disappointed. I didn't want to be anyone's replacement; I wasn't sure I wanted to be a social worker. I still dreamed of being a singer-songwriter, and were there other possibilities in my future? Did I want to be continually asking the advice of a spirit when I was starting to relish my independence? Wouldn't that be like having my mom around all the time? However, I didn't say anything, not wanting to hurt his feelings.

Another time, we did a telepathy experiment.

"I'm going to think of a scene, and I'd like you to tell me what you see," he instructed.

In colours more vivid than those I generally visualize, I saw a young Egyptian girl, simply dressed, sitting in a small boat. She was paddling toward the shore. Long reeds were poking out of the waters of the Nile. When she finally reached the shore, she walked toward a cave-like structure. The door, made of stone, opened before her. Inside was an older woman richly dressed. This woman smiled at her and pointed to a drawing—or was it a hieroglyph? —on the stone wall. She started to explain something. And that was it, other than throughout this vision, I heard the piping notes of a flute meandering aimlessly in a tuneless tune.

When I told Paul what I'd seen, he beamed at me. "That's exactly it. That young girl was you in a previous life, and the woman was your teacher. Only I'm puzzled about the music. I didn't project that."

"Well, seeing that I'm the musical person here, I must have supplied the accompaniment," I replied.

One Saturday morning, I was even more impressed. We were in my bed up to no good when all of a sudden, Paul reared up. "Get up—get dressed, right now!"

"What?" I stretched like a cat, lazy and luxuriant.

"Don't argue; get dressed—NOW!"

I scrambled for my clothes.

"Your friend Rosie is curious to see what I look like; and she's on her way here."

"But Paul, I always tell her not to disturb me when you're here. She's always respected that."

"Not this time. She will use the excuse of returning the pot you lent to her."

In seconds, we were fully dressed and sitting at my table. Knock-knock. I stared at Paul, unbelieving.

I got up, opened the door, and sure enough, there was Rosie, pot in hand.

"I just thought I'd return this pot," she said, glancing at Paul curiously. Paul nodded at her. "Oh, sorry for disturbing you."

"Well, since you're here, Rosie, this is my counsellor, Paul. Paul, this is my friend Rosie."

"Hellos" were politely said and soon, Rosie took her leave.

Paul and I almost collapsed with relief after the door closed behind her. What if Paul hadn't been forewarned?

Sometime later, things on the psychic front got even more interesting. Upon his arrival that Tuesday evening, Paul mentioned he was feeling very tired and asked if he could take a short nap.

"Of course."

Somehow, he managed to adjust his long body on my small couch at a very awkward angle. I sat across from him, sipping tea, wondering how he could drop off so quickly. Then, when he started speaking to me with his eyes closed, I almost dropped my mug.

"Fear not. It is I, Simon Peter," Paul proclaimed in a deep voice.

I gaped at him. "Paul?"

"No, it is I, Simon Peter, who speak through this man."

"Oh?"

"I am pleased that you have joined with him, for he is a true servant of God."

"Th— thank you."

"I am his guardian. He is aware of me, but there is something I must tell you which you must not tell him."

"Are you sure you should be telling me then?"

"Yes, I must tell you, for you are his soul mate."

I leaned forward.

"In his past life, he was John the Baptist."

"Oh."

"But you must never tell him." Peter then bade me a fond farewell.

I promised that I wouldn't tell him, but how weird was that? Paul had told me that since we were "one soul," we were never to keep any secrets from each other, yet here I was conspiring with his guardian to keep Paul in the dark about his past life!

Paul woke up refreshed. I told him what had occurred.

"Oh, so you met Peter, did you?" he said jovially as if Peter was a fishing buddy. "And what did he have to say?"

I decided that discretion was the better part of valour. "He, uh, is happy that we're together and said you're a good guy."

"That's nice. Now would you like to meet your guardian?"

"You mean I have one, too?'

"Of course, and a very powerful one."

Now I was getting excited.

Paul shut his eyes, resuming his "sleep." At length, a higher-pitched voice spoke through him—but it still sounded like Paul.

"Greetings, Elizabeth. It is I, your guardian, Jeanne d'Arc! I wish you to know that I am always watching over you. You must always be brave and have courr-rajh!" Whereupon the blessed saint bid me adieu.

The nuns would be green with envy if only they could hear this declaration, but the spoilsport in my mind was already asking, *is that French accent for real?* I couldn't picture myself having Joan of Arc as a guardian. Maybe if I joined the army? For that matter, I was skeptical about Paul's past life as John the Baptist. How many others had made that claim? Wasn't there another guy I'd read about in a book about reincarnation?

However, a few years before I met Paul, I tried my hand at automatic writing with my mom as an enthusiastic witness. We went through several past lives. I was Nem, an Egyptian temple artist happily married to a cousin in my first life. I'd been a court jester to Henry IV of France, a nun, and then a peasant woman with eight children. Mom and I were twins in one life. In another, Mom eloped with a Mexican bandit. The life I was "paying for" was that of John Adair, a drunken sailor and writer of bad poetry. He had a woman in one of the islands by the name of Farina that I later learned later was a type of flour—F-L-O-U-R, not the other kind—not as romantic as it sounded. He died in a storm at sea.

My Baptist friend, Cathy, was highly suspicious of this activity. She warned me that Vera, my guide, could be the devil leading me astray. "It says in the Bible to test the spirits," she told me and promptly decided she was qualified to do this. On her next visit, she brought a Bible. She opened it and asked Vera all sorts of questions. The kicker was, "Do you believe that Jesus Christ is the only begotten Son of God?"

Cathy said demons hate that question and go crazy when asked. However, Cathy didn't know what to make of it when Vera calmly answered, "Yes."

I felt relieved that my head didn't go into a spin cycle, spewing vomit and swear words in seven different languages. Later I wondered what Cathy would have done if that happened. Would she have been expert enough to conduct an exorcism? Or would she run screaming out of the door, never to return, leaving my poor mom to clean up the mess and wash my mouth out with soap?

I never took this past-life exploration too seriously; for me it was an amusing experiment. I concluded that I was accessing a creative part of my mind. I had an active imagination and had read Lord knows how many books. Also, when I saw samples of automatic writing in library books, I noticed it changed according to the different "characters" the writer accessed; the writers wrote rapidly and without pause. On the other hand, my illegible scrawl remained the same no matter who was "on," and I frequently paused to figure out the answers. Sometime later, I read that Edgar Cayce, the granddaddy of all psychics, warned against the practice as it attracted lower spirits and could lead to insanity. I stopped.

Just one last thing. Like everyone in the psychic "who's who," I had allegedly been alive in the time of Jesus. As an innkeeper's wife, Johanna was too busy to be an active follower of Jesus, but the man and his message deeply touched her. Impulsively, I asked Vera if there was any mention of me in the Bible. She gave me the numbers of a chapter and verse. When I looked it up, the verse referred to a group of women who carried away the body of John the Baptist after his beheading.

Hmm . . .

(Weird spacey music)

14

My Mother was
My Love Rival

One Saturday evening, after a family dinner, Lita showed me the necklace Paul had given her. She had hung it up in her room from a hook in the wall like a decoration. I presumed he had not explained the meaning of the dark blue background! Paul had also given my mother a gift—a plate from a Dutch candy store, one of those with the funny sayings. *A man should be like coffee, hot, sweet, and strong.* Mom had it displayed on the mantelpiece in the living room for all to see. I felt uneasy. Why did he get her a plate with this particular saying?

It felt strange not to tell Mom what was happening in my life. I'd always shared everything with her before. Now I couldn't breathe a word. If anyone found out about Paul and me, it could end his career. It was heartbreaking, as Mom had always been my number-one person. Now our formerly deep talks were all just surface chatter.

Since Dad's death, Mom had bloomed. She wrote poetry both in Polish and English. A Polish newspaper in the United States published many of her poems and a few stories that she had submitted. On her own, she published a couple of booklets of her English poems. She liked to explore Eastern spiritual ideas long before the "new age" made it trendy. She held poetry and song circles at home. She welcomed literary friends as well as anyone who only wished to listen.

Of course, the first thing she asked me after supper was if I had worked on any new songs. So, I sang the one I'd written for Paul. She loved it and asked me to bring it to our next circle.

The following Tuesday night, Paul was silent as he sat at my table.

Finally, I had to draw him out. "Did you have a bad day?"

He sighed. "I'm disappointed in you, darling."

I was surprised. "How so?"

"You played my song for your mother."

"So?"

"You wrote that song for me. You weren't supposed to sing it for anyone else."

"What?!" I was flabbergasted. How can you keep a song, a poem, or anything of that nature locked in a closet and only perform it for one person? Authors often dedicate their books to individuals, still publishing them for everyone to read. I tried to explain this to him, but he didn't get it.

"You wrote that song for *me*!"

What else could I do? I apologized.

"I forgive you," he said, after a pause, "but I must say I'm disappointed!"

On my next visit to Mom, she drew me aside and said confidentially, "You know, I think Paul is interested in me as a woman. I don't think his marriage is a happy one. We find so much to talk about! I never thought I'd meet a man like him." She blushed like a young girl.

"Oh, really?" was all I could say; however, my emotions were on a spin cycle. *Oh, God! Mom is a beautiful woman. She probably has way more in common with Paul than I do. Hands off my man, bitch! Did I just call her a bitch? Feeling a black humour fit coming on. What a story this would make in a True Confessions magazine! My Mother was my Love Rival! Was Paul attracted to her? What did he mean by giving her that plate? Was he saying that he was hot, sweet, and strong? Oh, God, this is so embarrassing; Mom and me falling for the same man!*

"Paul has practically adopted all of us," Mom said dreamily. "He brings us small gifts. He told me we were all very special and like a second family to him, but I think that's only an excuse to see me."

The next time I saw Paul, I told him what Mom had said. Paul cringed.

"I don't know what to do. I haven't done anything to encourage her. Not a thing! You must believe me, darling!"

"Well, what about that plate you gave her? You know: *A man should be like coffee, hot, sweet, and strong.* Were you advertising?"

"It was a joke! She told me she was ready for a relationship. I like and respect her; she's a wonderful person, but you're the one I love."

In the end, I gave him the benefit of the doubt. Perhaps I'd read too much into it.

One Tuesday evening, Paul phoned to inform me that he couldn't come over. "I have the most violent headache, and it was your sister who caused it."

I couldn't believe it. I sometimes felt Lita was a pain but surely not that much of one. "My little sister gave you a headache?"

"And more!" he groaned. "I had a counselling appointment with your family today, and I thought perhaps I could psychically accelerate Lita's spiritual and emotional growth; a little unconventional, but nothing out of line. Your mother was there too, darling. So, I asked Lita to close her eyes and open her mind to me completely, and I placed my hands on her head. Never have I encountered such tremendous resistance. Then, after some time, I had to run to the bathroom and throw up. That has never happened to me before!"

"Oh, poor you," I sympathized.

What a stubborn little cuss Lita was!

The next time I saw my sister, she told me her side of the story. "Nobody, and I mean, nobody is going to mess with my head. I resisted him with everything I could and made him throw up!" She laughed triumphantly.

BWA-HA HA HAHA!

As things turned out, Lita was smarter than I was!

15

DANGER FROM THE EAST!

M om held her circles once a month. Her living room was filled with the usual gang of wannabe poets, storytellers, and one lone songwriter. Her British friend, Claire, wrote short stories, and another of her friends, Myra, wrote poetry; my pal, Cathy, was there too, along with her boyfriend, Raj, from India, and his pal, Samir. Raj was majoring in engineering, and his friend was pursuing a degree in Business Administration.

Earlier, Cathy had tried to fix me up with Samir. We had a picnic in her backyard that was aborted by wasps swarming over our food. Nothing came of it. However, at the end of each evening at Mom's, Samir asked me if he could give me a ride home. With my usual frostiness, I refused.

On this particular evening, Samir stood up for the first time and said he wanted to read a poem—dedicated to me! Now I can't remember whether he wrote it or quoted an author. It ran something like this but much more beautifully phrased than I have set down here.

If I were a little bird perched on a branch
where you sit in your garden
would you feed me a few crumbs,
and, after a time, if I returned,
would you extend your hand,
so I could perch on your finger?

When he finished reading it, everyone let out a collective sigh. Samir handed me the poem and remained standing in front of me, gazing at me with those soulful brown eyes, making himself vulnerable in front of all those people. I, the ice princess, was speedily defrosting into a puddle on Mom's carpet.

I wanted to cry out, *Yes, yes, yes! I'll buy you a ten-year supply of birdseed! I'll even build you a birdhouse! Take me—I'm yours!* But instead, I tucked the paper with the poem in my pocket, thanking him coolly and politely. Then, at the end of the evening, I again rudely refused Samir's offer of a lift home.

I remembered what Paul had told me. "There can be no secrets between us. There can be no secrets between soul mates." Thus, the next day, I told Paul of Samir's interest in me and about the poem he'd recited to me.

Indeed, Paul informed me that Mom had mentioned her concerns about my boorish behaviour toward such a charming young man. Understandably, she wondered if I didn't want to date him, could I not at least have behaved in a friendly manner?

"Let's see what your guardian says about this, darling." With that, Paul lapsed into one of his trances. The Maid of Orleans sounded frantic.

"THERE IS DANGER—DANGER FROM THE EAST!"

Danger to whom, I wonder. I doubt that Samir will suddenly transform into a knife-wielding maniac!

"YOU MUST CUT OFF CONTACT WITH THE EAST! THERE IS DANGER! DANGER FROM THE EAST!"

"This is very serious, darling," said Paul when he emerged from his trance. "There is only one way to deal with this danger. You must find this Samir's address, tear the poem into little pieces, and mail it back to him!"

NO, NO! my heart cried out. "Can't I keep it for when I'm an old lady?" I asked tentatively. "As a keepsake?"

Paul's eyes narrowed. "Your guardian warned you. There is something very untrustworthy about this man. If you keep the poem, he'll take it as encouragement. Trust me, if you do what I tell you, he'll never bother you again."

So, I did it. I did what Paul said, tore the poem into a thousand pieces, stuck them into an envelope, and chucked it into the mailbox. I felt sick about what I was doing. Samir didn't deserve this treatment from me. Afterwards, I cried and cried. Even now, fifty years later, I still cringe whenever I think back on that act of cruelty. I'm so, so, sorry, Samir.

Ironic, isn't it? I originally went for counselling to stop precisely this hurtful behaviour. Now Paul was inciting me to repeat it.

Paul was right about the outcome. Mom and I never saw Samir again. For the first time, I felt trapped. I wanted to fly, but my spiritual marriage with Paul clipped my wings.

As for Samir, some years later, Mom and I heard through the grapevine that he had married a woman from his culture and had two children. They moved to Calgary and were reportedly very happy. I was glad for Samir.

It would be a long time before I found true love and happiness.

16

Exile

P aul had an extra weeknight free and chose to spend it with me. On that particular Thursday evening, we were neither forewarned nor forearmed. St. Peter must have been off on a coffee break this time; while Paul and I were doing our thing, there was a knock on my door. The light shining from my window indicated that I was home.

As I pulled on a caftan, Paul cowered in the alcove. I opened the door with the chain on just a notch to see who it was—please, God, NO! There stood Mom, Lita, and Ray smiling at me expectantly.

"We were at loose ends, so we thought we'd drop in on you," said Mom. Dropping in was a regular thing with my family, and usually, I'd have been delighted to welcome them and put the kettle on. But, this time, it was clear I'd have to do some quick thinking.

"Um—I'm so sorry. I'm not feeling well. I have the most awful migraine headache."

"Oh, surely just for a little while," pleaded Mom. "We've walked all this way."

"No. I'm not feeling well. I need to lie down."

"I could give you a neck and shoulder rub," offered Mom.

"No!" I said more forcefully than I would have liked.

Lita was shifting from one foot to the other. "Aw, come on, sis!"

Damn it, why don't they LEAVE? "I'm sorry. I'm going to close the door now. I need to lie down. And in the future, would you please phone me before you come." I didn't wait for a reply, didn't look at my mother's face as I firmly shut the door. I winced as I pictured her dejection, sensing neediness in her tonight that wasn't usually there. Usually, she seemed so self-sufficient. *Damn it, why did they have to come on a night when Paul was here?*

When I heard their footsteps moving away, I finally let out a breath. Paul emerged from the alcove fully dressed. He flopped on the couch. We stared at each other. It was too close a call.

He groaned. "If anyone ever found out, I'd be ruined. So, you're going to have to move, darling. Find an apartment with a controlled entrance and not within walking distance of your family."

I agreed. Paul had his family, job, and reputation to think of. God knew I wasn't out to ruin his life.

A couple of months later, I found myself in this lovely third-floor bachelor suite—immaculate and white, with parquet floors and up-to-the-minute appliances in the clean kitchenette. There was even a balcony, though I couldn't say much for the view of the front entrance and parking lot.

All I had for furniture was a kitchen table with four chairs and a coffee table, which I purchased second-hand. A large mattress sprawled on the floor against one wall; I disguised it with my Indian bedspread and colourful cushions to give it a cozier appearance. Along another wall, Paul had put together a bookshelf constructed of cement blocks and wooden planks, three deep. Finally, I covered the main living area with a golden nine-by-twelve carpet.

There was no Rosie just across the hall in this large building, nor friendly conversations with the caretaker's wife on the stair landing. Invisible hands surely cleaned this place, for I never caught anyone vacuuming or dusting in the hallway. There was no old man on the first floor to say "hi" to; he always had his door open and watched folks come in and go out. A sociable fellow, Rosie and I had frequently spent a few minutes chatting with him.

Here, instead, was an elevator with people averting their faces if I happened to intrude on their space. In the laundry room, located in the bowels of the basement, I rarely ran into anyone.

My new digs were located across the bridge in a semi-industrial area, "on the wrong side of the tracks." Many Armed Forces members and their families lived there. Most of the houses at that time were pretty run down. I'd go for walks and occasional suppers at the nearby fish and chip store but felt no attachment to this neighbourhood.

On Saturdays, I could walk to town, but on the way, I passed light industrial buildings and railroad tracks. There was nothing pretty to look at. I thought of the bridge as the border between towns with all my friends and family on the other side. Whenever I did visit, I felt hollow. Accustomed to long, soul-satisfying heart-to-heart talks, now it was all superficiality about the weather, how things were going on the job, and "seen any good movies lately?" I would return from these visits feeling lonelier than ever.

Paul had a copy of my key so he could come over any time he wanted. He called my place his "home away from home." However, many times when I returned from work, I'd just want to be on my own. I never knew when he'd be there. I was tired of pretending to be bright and cheerful when I felt so rotten.

After some weeks, Paul expressed his concern for me. "Darling, you haven't had an orgasm for a long time. We must talk about this."

Really? He is worried about my orgasms?

So, I told him about how isolated I was feeling from friends and family and not being too thrilled in general about the area where I lived.

"Oh, you poor dear! I must make up for this in some way. We've never gone out together. I'll start taking you out."

"Aren't you worried about getting discovered, Paul?" *Isn't that why I moved here?*

"Oh, we'll be discreet."

Our first outing was to this romantic restaurant. The decor was pure Hawaiian fantasy. The ceiling was dark, with tiny little lights shining like stars. There were tropical plants and an indoor stream. The basket-weave chairs had high, rounded backs. Soft pink tablecloths graced the tables along with gleaming glassware and spotless cutlery. They had even artfully arranged the napkins. Their specialty was the Hawaiian buffet. I should have been elated. Instead, all I did was hope that Paul didn't act too lover-like. Our age difference seemed so obvious; people would think he was my dad. I didn't hold onto his arm as we came in, nor did I reach for his hand across the table. Our conversation was stilted and primarily focused on the food.

"You're not feeling comfortable, are you?" Paul said after a while.

I shook my head.

"It's our age difference, isn't it?"

I nodded, feeling ashamed. *Age shouldn't matter,* I told myself, but it did to me—very much so.

"That's entirely normal, darling. Of course, there is quite a difference in our ages; as we go out more, you'll get used to it."

But you know what? I never did. No matter how guilty I felt about not displaying affection in public, I never held hands with him on our walks to the park or along a quiet beach.

One time, Paul had a few days free. "Let's get away for a short trip, darling. There's a nice hotel where we can stay, a lovely resort a few hours away from the city. Nobody will know us there."

From the moment we started on our way, I developed the most vicious headache. When we booked into the hotel, I had Paul sign me up for a separate room next to his.

Although I slept with him in his bed, both mornings, bright and early, I returned to my room, rumpled up the bed covers, and dented the pillow to make it look like I slept in my bed. God forbid that the cleaning staff should guess we were lovers! I would surely die of embarrassment!

My headache lasted the whole three days.

Paul tried his healing-hands technique several times to get rid of it with no result, which surprised him. "I'm usually very successful with my healing," he'd say. I guess he never figured out that our being together was the real cause of the headache. Only when we returned to my apartment did it "miraculously" heal.

One day, I came back home from work and found him lying on my mattress, staring at the ceiling.

"You look like you're feeling down. Did you have a bad day?" I asked.

"Oh, not too bad."

I could tell he was being evasive. "What's been happening with you, Paul?"

He sighed. "Oh, nothing much. I've just been a little depressed lately."

I stroked his forehead. "Anything I can do to help you feel better?"

"Well—" he drew the word out reluctantly. "Well, there is one thing," he said, as his eyes shifted sideways. "I don't know if you'd be willing to do it. But, of course, you don't have to." He sighed.

"What is it?"

"If you would meet me for lunch, say every Tuesday and Thursday, that would make me feel better."

My stomach curled into a tight ball. "But I work on those days."

"That's all right. I'd meet you at the entrance, and we could drive down to the beach a few blocks down the road and have our lunch there."

I fell silent. My work had so far remained unaffected by my romantic ups and downs. I knew from a recent evaluation that my boss thought I was doing a good job; he had even rated my performance as "excellent" in some areas. My workplace was the only normal, uncomplicated part of my life. I was in turmoil. *But my workplace is downtown. We could get discovered. How is that being discreet? Why are you asking this of me? Aren't you worried about running into someone you know? And what if Louise finds out? I thought you didn't want to hurt her!*

Paul sensed my reluctance. "Oh, that's all right, darling. You don't have to do anything. I'll manage." He retreated into gloomy silence, sighing ever so often. He didn't want any supper when I offered to make him some. I didn't feel much like eating, either.

He looked so hurt. I felt bad for him, guilty for making him suffer. Reluctantly, I agreed to his request.

His recovery was instantaneous. Immediately he sprang up to make us some sandwiches for supper. "Now I feel much better, thanks to you, darling." Paul ate heartily.

My sandwich remained untouched, but he didn't notice that.

17

My Ordeal

I read a western novel about natives capturing some of the pioneers. The natives would stand in a double line with just enough space for one person to walk or run through. Each tribe member possessed a club or weapon. As each unfortunate victim faced the ordeal of walking through this narrow passage, the tormentors would strike, stab, or otherwise injure him. I didn't realize that I was about to go through an ordeal of my own, but I soon found out.

Every Tuesday and Thursday, I'd leave my office a few minutes ahead of the others and walk down the long hallway of the building. Office doors on either side would open and close as government employees streamed out for their lunch break. With my heart pounding, I'd glance nervously left, right, and behind to see if my co-workers followed me. Finally, at the end of that infinitely long passage to the entrance, stood Paul, beaming at me.

We'd pile into his humble mud-coloured Toyota and head for the beach, where he'd park the car along the curb. The routine never varied. Bag lunches first; then, he'd pin me in an adolescent grip, kissing me passionately. Here it was broad daylight, and, as far as I knew, many civil servants would take their lunch around here in the fair weather.

Mentally I cringed. *Why am I doing this?*

After a few weeks, the shit hit the fan.

"Who was that man I saw you kissing goodbye at the entrance? An uncle or some other relative?" asked Ann, the senior secretary.

I blushed. "Uh—no." I didn't bother to enlighten her but resumed my typing.

She gazed at me with narrowed eyes.

That afternoon when I came into the staff room, Ann and Jane were already seated at the table.

"Seems Elizabeth has a boyfriend," she drawled. "Kind of old for her, though. Wonder where she found him? In a lonely-hearts ad?"

"Probably met him in an old people's home," added Jane snidely.

I waxed and waned, hot and cold in turns. Finally, inadvertently, my trembling hand dropped the cup of hot water in which I was about to brew my tea. I pretended not to hear them and wiped the floor before walking out. However, the expression on my face must have told them that they had found an easy target. I spent at least ten minutes trying to pull myself together in the washroom. When I returned to my desk, I said nothing to anyone and tried my utmost to concentrate on my work.

But the staff room debacle wasn't enough for Ann, and she made good and sure to spread the gossip to the outer office, and, from that time on, never a day passed without her and her devotees making some cruel quips. One time, I remember typing a detailed report while she and three other women stood in front of my desk talking about "love in bloom" and "May and December romance" and how sweet it all was; though it was a crying shame that a girl like me couldn't latch on to someone her age.

I'm not seeing them. I'm not hearing them, I kept telling myself, grimly ignoring them, and continuing my work. I was so shaky I couldn't vouch for the accuracy of that particular report.

Going in to work each morning, I felt as if I was passing through hostile territory. My throat constricted, my solar plexus was a wall of fear, and my hands felt cold. I would hurry by my tormentors with a quick "good morning," and I no longer joined in conversations or friendly bantering.

Sometimes, a deep inner knowing will rise at such times. Instinctively, I knew that the other women, left to themselves, would not instigate this mental cruelty—they were following Ann's lead. Ann had chosen to make herself my enemy. But why? Had her husband left her for a younger woman, causing her to heap her bitter harvest upon me?

At the time, community education primarily consisted of the creative arts, French and Chinese cooking, and ballroom dancing. They didn't offer assertive training courses. I was too scared to tell the bitches off. And what if my boss got wind of what was going on?

I phoned in sick a lot. Indeed, I felt totally exhausted from lack of sleep and couldn't face going to the office. In those days, I believe there was no such thing as "stress leave"; I had to endure.

Whenever I would tell Paul about the office gossip, he'd try to cheer me up by inventing a story about a timid sparrow picked upon by a flock of wicked magpies. And then, when the Great Spirit, in His infinite compassion, turned the sparrow into an eagle, the magpies knew they were nothing beside her and flew away, never to return.

"Just remember that you're on a higher spiritual plane, darling. Ignore them, and soon they'll stop harassing you. You'll see."

Only they never did.

My guide, Joan of Arc, urged me to "be brave, my child" and "always have COURR-RAJ!"

One evening, as I peeled an orange, chewed a few segments, and threw the rest away, I realized with a shock that was the only thing I had eaten all day. Even one or two bites of food felt like too much. Formerly a curvy size 12 drawing whistles from construction workers, I had shrunk to a skinny size eight.

This weight loss earned me no compliments. My mother and close friends were concerned, noting my pale face and the dark circles under my eyes. I rarely said anything and when I did, I spoke in a monotone.

"I know something terrible is troubling you," Mom told me. "If you can't confide in me, talk about it to Paul, for heaven's sake. It's killing you."

Talk about it to Paul—Ha Ha!

One day, Mr. Phillips, my boss, said he wanted to talk to me. On his desk, I saw that he had my personnel file open. "Please sit down," he said kindly. He studied the file and then cleared his throat. "Elizabeth, in the past year, you were doing excellent work; however, in the last couple of months, the quality of your performance has dropped drastically."

I stared down at my lap.

"Do you have an explanation about what could have caused such a change?"

I said nothing. What could I tell him? *Your sadistic senior secretary and her cronies are making my life a total hell? I'm trapped in a spiritual marriage with a married man old enough to be my father?*

"Is there something happening in your personal life?"

"Yes," I replied. "But I can't talk about it."

"I thought it might be something like that." He gazed at me sympathetically. "Try to focus more on your work, will you?"

Back in my apartment, I broke the news to Paul. "Paul, I've just been given the worst job evaluation ever because of those bitches! I can't take it anymore. I'm sorry, love, but I'll no longer be meeting you for lunch."

"I see," he murmured. "Well, of course, darling, if you say so." He stared at the plateful of fried sausage and canned peas and carrots. Then, glumly, he pushed the plate away. "I'm not feeling well. I need to lie down for a while if you don't mind."

He lay down on my mattress and shortly fell "asleep." Now, why wasn't I surprised when St. Peter came through all at once?

"HOW DARE YOU TREAT THIS SERVANT OF GOD SO SHABBILY! YOU, WHO HAVE COMMITTED YOURSELF TO BE A HELP-MEET TO AID HIM IN HIS SPIRITUAL ENDEAVOURS!"

What spiritual endeavours? Have we ever talked about the Bible or attended church services? Have we med- itated together, even once? Did we perform "good works" such as "feeding the hungry" or "clothing the naked"?

Also, where was Joan of Arc when I needed her? Alas, the Maid of Orleans didn't utter a peep. Mind you, wouldn't that have been quite a show? Old St. Pete berating me in his booming voice and Joan blasting HIM in my defence in her awful accent! But perhaps that would be too difficult for Paul to accomplish! However, even the Rock of Christendom failed to persuade me.

Paul left soon after with a headache.

18

A Sad, Bad End

"Promise me you'll never leave me!"

I gazed at Paul with dead eyes. "I promise I'll never leave you."

"You must promise three times. Promise me again that you'll never leave me."

"I promise that I'll never leave you," I repeated dully.

"Now—one more time."

I sighed. "I promise I'll never leave you."

Paul perked up at once. "That makes me feel so much better, darling."

I was silent. I had trouble believing my own false words because breaking up had been very much on my mind, only I kept brushing the thought away, rather than facing the inevitable big scene.

A few days later, I was having a particularly awful time at work. The crowning denouement happened at the photocopier. I was in charge of the pesky machine, and now there was a paper jam. The line of people was growing; everyone was impatient to copy their documents. As hard as I tried, I couldn't for the life of me get that paper out. My hands started to tremble, and tears formed in my eyes. In front of me stood Ann, arms folded, with a smile on her face. She kept on staring at me, staring, staring, staring, and smiling.

I started to shake and immediately left the mess for someone else to fix. Then, murmuring to my boss that I wasn't feeling well, I took off early. I caught the Number 23 bus, hardly noticing the scenery, as it turned onto Bridge Street, passed the Sally Ann, crossed the bridge, drove by the light industrial buildings and railway tracks, and finally stopped close to the front of my building. Today was Tuesday. I knew Paul would be there, cooking up the invariable "steakette" with instant mashed potatoes and frozen green beans.

"Paul, I have to tell you something," I blurted out when I came through the door.

"Can't it wait till after supper? I'm just in the middle of cooking."

"No, it has to be now. Turn off the stove."

Paul sighed and stepped out onto the main living area, mildly impatient. "What is it, darling?"

I cut to the chase. "Our relationship is no longer working for me. It's over."

He stared at me incredulously. "What did you say?"

"I'm saying we're through. I can't take all the secrecy and isolation, and those bitches are constantly harassing me at work."

Paul stepped closer. "But this can't be. Just a few days ago you promised—you promised me *three times* that you would never leave me!"

I closed my eyes wearily. "Well, I'm sorry, Paul, but I am leaving you."

"NO, NO, NO, NO!"

In a flash, he was down on the floor—this tall six-foot-two man, this counsellor-shaman-psychic-veteran—thrashing his arms and legs up and down like a two-year-old.

"NO, NO, NO! YOU CAN'T DO THIS! YOU CAN'T DO THIS TO ME!"

Was I really seeing what I was seeing?

All at once, he jumped up and grabbed my arm! My God, had the man lost his sanity? I became aware of how much stronger he was than me.

"Kneel!" he ordered. "And stay there!"

I knelt. *Please, God, I want this to be over.*

Paul frantically searched through my bookshelf. It didn't take him long to find what he wanted. Holding the Bible in his hands, he charged back to where I knelt. "Put your right hand on the Bible," he commanded. "Can't you hear God calling your name? Can't you hear God telling you that we are to be together—forever?"

I pretended to listen, but of course, besides the panicky rise and fall of my breathing, I heard nothing. "No, I hear nothing."

"But you MUST—you MUST! Don't you hear him, darling? He's calling your name! He's talking to you RIGHT NOW!"

I shook my head. "No, I don't hear a thing."

"YOU'RE NOT LISTENING TO HIM! YOU'RE NOT LISTENING TO HIM!" Paul paced up and down. "YOU MUST LISTEN!"

Silently I rose to my feet. "Paul, I want you to leave now."

Instead, he seized me and carried me to my mattress. I felt the weight of his body crushing me, his tongue seeking my resistant mouth. I forced myself to go completely limp.

This was no lover's kiss; only a tongue probing the inside of my mouth.

When he finally stopped, he looked down at me and pleaded, "But hasn't our sex life always been good, darling?"

"It has been," I admitted, for that much was true. "But sex is not the issue. My sanity is. Now get off me and leave. Please, just leave!"

Slowly he rose again. "You can't do this to me—to us!"

I snapped. "IF YOU DON'T GET OUT OF HERE, IMMEDIATELY, I'LL CALL THE POLICE! AND I WANT MY KEYS BACK RIGHT NOW!"

Paul glared at me, his formerly pale face turning a bright red. "ALL RIGHT! I'M GOING ALREADY! AND HERE ARE YOUR DAMNED KEYS!"

Flinging them at me, Paul stomped and slammed his way out of the building shouting God-knew-what as he left. The neighbours must have surely gotten an earful.

Instead of feeling relieved, I felt like I'd been bombed inside. I knew I could not be alone that night. So, I phoned a friend, confessed all, and stayed several days at her place. (Thank you, Cindy.)

A few days later, I gave a month's notice to my landlord that I'd be moving. I found a nice bachelor apartment on the other side of the bridge, a short walking distance from my family. Even though I didn't tell her what had occurred, I wanted my mommy.

19

Boomerang

As a volunteer on the Crisis Line, I sometimes talked to women who'd been beaten. I felt great empathy. Having witnessed my mother's experience, I hoped they would move on with their lives, but many of them returned to their abusers. Even though my body didn't bear any physical scars, I went back to Paul.

Why?

Because he was *there*. He was *always* there!

Whenever my mother invited me for a family dinner, Paul was there, acting as what, the positive male role model, the "Pater Familias," of his very special adopted family? As ever, he entertained us with his wit and deep-sounding wisdom.

At Lita's 15th birthday party, he was there.

When a whole gang of us went up to a local beach resort, guess who Mom invited to pop up for a day?

One time Paul pulled me aside. "The knife," he whispered. "You must bury it! It's dangerous!"

I stared at him incredulously. "Can't I just give it back to you?"

He shook his head.

"I actually have to bury it?"

"You MUST do so as soon as possible—it's dangerous!" he repeated.

Seriously? How would I do that? It felt like a silly
thing to do. Besides, where would I dig a hole? On the front
lawn of my new apartment building? In a city park? In Mom's
back yard?

*"Hi, Mom, can I borrow your shovel? I just need to
bury something in your garden. No, never mind what it is!
Just give me that damned shovel!"*

So, I didn't bury it. I thought of donating the knife
to the Goodwill store, but the idea made me shudder. Who
would buy an actual hunting knife, and what would they do
with it? Would they do something harmful? No, I didn't want
that. Instead, I pitched it into the large bin behind my apartment building, relieved to be rid of the thing.

Years later, I learned from reading up on occult subjects that objects with bad energy should be buried so the
earth could render them harmless. On the day of our "spiritual
wedding," we had placed two curses on that knife. Therefore,
to Paul's way of thinking, the knife, which represented his
soul, was now cursed and very dangerous. A possible alternative would have been to throw it into the ocean—as water
and salt combined are purifiers.

But what did I know of such things back then? So,
when Paul asked if I had gotten rid of it, I nodded "yes," not
telling him how. He seemed relieved.

As I said, he was still a looming presence in my life.
Paul, Paul, always there, sitting in the family chair!

He was so much like the man I fell in love with, that
I started to doubt myself. Also, there was still a sexual pull.
So, yes, I let him back into my life once again. This time,
however, I had conditions.

a) *I never wanted to hear from St. Peter and Joan of Arc ever again.*

b) *We could never meet for lunch. Mr. Phillips transferred me to a different department. I wanted no trace of gossip or harassment to mar my fresh start.*

c) *I would tell Mom that we were together so she wouldn't misconstrue his frequent family presence.*

d) *He'd consider getting a vasectomy; I was worried about side effects from the birth control pills.*

Much to my surprise, Paul agreed to these terms, and just like that, we were a going concern once again.

20

Mother Love

I was shaking in my boots when I arrived at Mom's house with the news of my relationship with Paul; scared and ashamed and full of dread.

How would she react? Would she hate me? There were several ways she could have responded.

TOTAL FURY!

"WHAT? I'M GOING TO RAISE HOLY HELL WITH THAT RAT BASTARD! HOW DARE HE SEDUCE MY DAUGHTER! I NEVER WANT TO SEE THAT SLIMEBALL AROUND HERE AGAIN!"

Yes, she could have said that, or:

"AND YOU! ALL THIS TIME, YOU'VE BEEN LYING TO ME! SNEAKING AROUND WITH A MARRIED MAN! YOU SHOULD BE ASHAMED!"

She could have played the "guilt" card. (Sobbing and snivelling)

> *"If you stabbed me in the heart, you couldn't find a worse way to hurt me. I can't believe you kept this from me! You knew I was in love with him, but you just let me go*

on thinking that he returned my feelings. I feel like such a fool! How could you do this to me!"

OR—WORST OF ALL!

"GET OUT! YOU'RE NO LONGER MY DAUGHTER; YOU'RE DEAD TO ME!"

To the best of my memory, this is what happened.

We were alone in her house, sitting at the kitchen table with a pot of tea at hand and a plate of cookies, untouched by me.

"Mom, I've got something to tell you." I swallowed. "It's really hard for me to tell you this."

"Go on," urged Mom kindly. "I've known for some time that something's been eating you."

"Um, for the past year, Paul and I have been together as a couple, and it's been practically killing me to keep it a secret from you. Also, him being married and all; well, it's been complicated."

Seeing the stunned look on her face was like a punch in my gut.

"I don't know what to think," she said hesitantly. "This is such a shock!"

"I'm so sorry, Mom. I didn't mean to hurt you."

"I need a little time to—to absorb this. So, give me a little time."

I nodded, collected my coat and left. *I hope Mom won't hate me!*

Let me tell you something about my mother. She had been attending Al-Anon meetings for almost ten years by this time. On her bedroom wall hung a framed cross-stitch of the Serenity Prayer.

God, grant me the serenity to accept
the things I cannot change
Courage to change the things I can
And the wisdom to know the difference

The following week, Mom phoned me. Quietly she informed me that she had decided to accept this situation. She wasn't happy about it, but she didn't want to lose me. "You'll always be my daughter!"

"Oh, Mom, I love you so much," I said tearfully. I was so grateful to her and for her.

I don't know if she spoke with Paul about our relationship. He was still allowed to visit Mom's home, but I noticed she was far more guarded with him, tolerating him for the sake of her straying daughter.

Mother love.

I'm happy to report that Mom did find love four years later. She met Stefan at a dance held at the Polish Hall. Stefan was also from Warsaw and respectably employed as an accountant. He spoke several languages and was an avid collector of jokes.

Stefan and Mom were together for 35 years.

21

The Second Time Around

Things were somewhat better the second time around. Our relationship was no longer a secret from my mother, and I attended Al-Anon meetings. I now had a "sponsor" with whom I could talk about my situation. That certainly took some of the weight off my shoulders.

However, one thing did not change. I was still embarrassed about our age difference.

One evening, Paul told me that his daughter-in-law Linda had come to visit him with his three-year-old granddaughter, Suzy. "Since we're soul mates, darling, I must tell you everything."

I braced myself.

"Linda confessed to me that she married my son because she was in love with me, and that was her way of getting closer to me." Seeing my eyes widen, he hastily added, "Oh, but she's a wonderful wife to Bill; you mustn't think ill of her!"

WHOA!

"Anyway, today, we took a long walk in the park. Linda said she was so happy to be with me, and she took me by the hand as we walked." He paused to gauge my reaction.

"Oh," I said blandly, feeling anything but bland.

"Several years ago, I told her about the woman of my dreams."

"You mean 'Helen,'" I interjected dryly, remembering the first time he kissed me and called me by that name.

"Yes, and today she asked me if she could fill that role for me."

WHAT?!

"Of course, I told her all about you, and she said she was happy for me. She said you must be a wonderful person." He looked at me a moment. "I had to tell you what happened with Linda, darling. There can be no secrets between us."

I eyed him warily.

Is he telling me this story to point out there are other fish in the sea even if there's snow on his roof? And didn't this Linda, his daughter-in-law, care about the effect her bombshell offer would have on her husband and mother-in-law? What would happen to little Suzy? Boy, if this were a soap opera, no one would believe it! Truth is certainly stranger than fiction!

Paul told me of a family he was counselling. "You should meet them, darling. The father is 69, and his wife is 36; they have a wonderful marriage. The problem is with their 13-year-old son, who's embarrassed by having a dad who looks like his grandfather. Would you like to meet them? I can arrange it."

Yikes! How would he introduce me? "This is my girl-friend who's embarrassed about our age difference." Was the wife then supposed to set an example for me? Did he want the four of us to socialize?

One day, Paul said, "I told my son about you."

"Oh? How did he react."

"He was concerned about me. He said that he'd kill you if you ever hurt me."

I said nothing.

Our relationship slid quietly downhill.

Paul was not insensitive to my mood. One November night, he said, "This isn't working out for you, is it? I guess the best thing for you is for me to leave."

I said nothing, tears filling my eyes.

Quietly he left.

Oh, thank you—thank you—thank you, Paul. This act was so unselfish of him. I felt so relieved.

Three hours later, my door opened. It was Paul—back again! He embraced me. "I went for a long drive and parked near some woods. I walked around outside in the snow, and everything was so beautiful. The snow was glistening. The moon was full, and I looked up at the stars, and I thought, it cannot possibly be that you and I can ever be apart, for we are one soul. And in that moment, I knew—I KNOW—that we are meant to be together."

I felt like a yo-yo, or a puppet on strings, being pulled up and then down, down, down, at the hands of a master puppeteer. In the days following, I vacillated. Should I stay? Should I go? *But he's been so good to me; he kept all his promises. How can I hurt him again? Worst of all, he even went through a vasectomy for me. Isn't that proof of his love? Oh, God, what am I going to do?*

How long I would have gone on like this, I don't know. Then, unwittingly, Paul himself precipitated the final blow to our relationship.

It was December, and we had just put up a ceiling-high natural Christmas tree in my living room. It was stunning, laden with lovely silver and white balls, silver garlands, tinsel, and other ornaments matching the silver and white theme. The top boasted a silver star. White lights created a soft, warm glow that filled the apartment.

We were admiring our handiwork when Paul said out of the blue, "You know, darling, I've been very selfish, expecting love and loyalty from you but being unwilling to make a full commitment to you; so, here's what I'm going to do. After the new year, I'm going to tell Louise that I want a divorce, and then we can get married legally!"

"I— I don't know what to say," I stuttered.

Paul took that as a "yes." He looked so happy.

Oh my God, I want to die. What have I done?

What I had meant to be a brief and beautiful romance had become oppressive. If only I had said a firm "no" to our "spiritual wedding," I would not have led him on, and I wouldn't be in such dire straits.

Nightmarish fantasies bloomed in my mind. I'd be a stepmom to Paul's kids, who were older than me. They'd hate me, and with good reason. I'd have broken Louise's heart and would also have to keep a watchful eye on Linda! My life would no longer be my own. Everything would be about him—his wants, his needs, his tastes—my youth and all my dreams stolen from me!

NO, NO, NO, NO!

I did the deed just after Christmas. I told him very quietly, what he denied within himself, that I could not possibly marry him, and I needed to end our relationship—for good.

This time, our breakup was quiet and non-dramatic. Paul stayed with me one more night, and that was it. Our last goodbye.

A few weeks later, I was astounded to receive a phone call at work from a woman who introduced herself as Paul's daughter, Karen. She told me that her parents truly had an unhappy marriage, and her dad was heartbroken about losing me; she hoped I would reconsider.

Regretfully, I told her that I needed to be on my own now. I wished her well.

One month later, Paul phoned me at my workplace.

"I'm phoning from the Essondale Hospital." He paused. "I've had two electric shock treatments."

I could feel him waiting, wishing, hoping; however, my 12-step meetings had taught me that taking care of myself is my first priority.

"I'm sorry to hear that, Paul," I replied. "I wish you well, but I can do nothing about it. So, please don't ever phone me again."

So sad. I felt so sad but oh so relieved and drained, totally drained, unable to do anything outside of my job. I was a wounded fox hiding out in her cave.

I've finally done the right thing. I've asked God for forgiveness. Paul is no longer welcome at Mom's. Surely now my life can go back to the way it was before, can't it? And surely my guitar, so long unused, can once again respond to my fingers, to new songs and music that I'll create! And once again, I'll dance along to Cat Stevens, won't I?

But no, it would be years before I would sing and dance again.

As for the Christmas tree, it was a skeletal remnant of its former glory. Brown pine needles littered the carpet. It was now a fire hazard—in late March.

22

MADNESS

Scenes from an Unquiet Mind

I

I'm lying on my bed in this small stuffy bachelor suite. It is 3:30 am, and I haven't slept. The knives are in the kitchenette, in a drawer where I've put them away to be safe. What if I were to get up, open the drawer, take out the biggest, sharpest knife, and ...stab myself ...in the right eye? The thought keeps coming back and back again. Finally, I get up, creep to the counter, pick up my eyeglasses, put them on, and return to bed. How stupid is this? Wouldn't it be embarrassing if I die in the night, and they find me wearing my glasses?

Yet, I feel better, as if wearing these glasses provides a form of protection, and I do drift into a troubled sleep. The next morning, I somehow manage to dress and drag myself to work.

II

I'm with a good friend alongside the ocean. We are strolling on a cement walkway far above the water. There are *no fences or rails along the sides. Suddenly, I think, "What if I push her, send her flying over the edge?" The urge feels so strong. Oh, God, what am I thinking? So, I make up an excuse, a flimsy reason to cut off our time together, and go home.*

Such thoughts also occur when I'm out with other friends. I'm scared to death of myself!

III

I've just finished reading an article about the University of Texas tower shooting in August 1966. After stabbing his wife and mother in their respective homes, Charles Whitman, a former marine, gathered up firearms and took them to the observation deck at the Main Building tower. Over the 96 minutes, he randomly fired at and killed 15 people and injured 31 others. The incident ended when a policeman and a civilian reached Whitman and shot him dead. His autopsy revealed that a tumour found in the white matter above his amygdala may have caused his violent tendencies.

With all these violent urges I've been experiencing, is it possible that I also have a tumour? Will I end up killing people? I'll kill myself first! The only tumour that needs expunging from my brain is you, Paul!

V

Over and over, I try to pray. "God, please heal me! Please, please! Please! I'm so sorry for what I did. Please, forgive me!" But no comfort comes to me in my darkness, not even the slightest glimmer of light. God has abandoned me.

VI

Damn you, Paul; you and your so-called "spiritual" wedding! I can't believe I took part in this travesty! What was I thinking? STUPID, STUPID, STUPID! Now I'm being punished. Well, I hope you're happy, Paul. Your curses seem to be working just fine, but the biggest curse in my life is YOU! I wish you had never been born!

VII

How will I get through this day of endlessly typing letters, reports, and documents and directing phone calls to the right people? The day grinds on eternally long. I want to burst out of my skin.

In the afternoon, my new boss calls me in. He's not happy with me. For one thing, I have a rotten attitude with my perpetually long face, I space out, and for another, I make far too many mistakes in my work.

"SHAPE UP OR SHIP OUT!" he tells me bluntly.

With all the effort I can muster, I focus, focus, focus, and do "shape up." Each morning, I slide a smiling persona over my long face. It works but takes up all my energy.

VIII

Back at home, I collapse in on myself. I'm a rag doll crumpled in a heap on my corner bed.

One evening, a friend comes over to pick me up for a movie.

"Before we go, could I please use your bathroom?" she asks.

I try to stall her. "If we don't leave now, we'll be late for the show."

But no. She has to do her business right NOW! So off she goes.

I am waiting for it. Then it comes.

"OH MY GOD!" She emerges from the poop pit, rolling her eyes. "Did I just see what I thought I saw?!"

I flush. *My bathtub is full of my greasy, unwashed dishes, which I had been squirrelling away. Unfortunately, I have no shower curtain to conceal them. Thus, my dirty little secret is revealed.*

We look at each other and shriek. I laugh so hard my stomach hurts.

IX

Sara Lee's cheesecake is my new best friend; so rich and velvety. Sweet, but not too sweet. I can't get enough of it. I eat and eat and eat until I feel I'm about to burst. I'm too full. Got to get rid of it. The toilet beckons, and I kneel before it. Afterwards, I feel like I'm SO disgusting. Who does this kind of thing? I never heard of anyone doing this. It's so gross. I'm so ashamed of myself, but I'm totally caught up in this decadence. Sara Lee, cookies, ice cream, and popcorn fill the dark, dismal void within—at least for a little while. The toilet is my new altar. Penitence is my new sacrament. Through my fault, through my fault, through my most grievous fault.

X

Where once my mind filled with music and lyrics, dreams, and optimism, it is now flat-lining. However, I do manage to eke out one song and that's it—my last hurrah. My creativity, once my greatest joy, is buried in the darkest recesses of my sick mind. I hide my guitar in the closet. I can't bear to look at it.

I hate being alone with my madness. Whenever AA hold a dance, they invite people from Al-Anon to attend. That's where I meet Ron. He has been sober for three years. When I ask him if he's married, he tells me he is divorced. Good! I don't want to make the same mistake twice, so when he asks me for a date, I agree to see him. Sadly, I drifted into yet another dysfunctional relationship.

Ron is so rude. When we're walking downtown, he often stares at other young women and comments on their assets. I tell him his behaviour is offensive. He insists that I'm jealous since I'm in love with him.

"I hate to say this," I say, "but I don't love you."

"Oh, yes you do—you're just in denial."

Always, he thinks he knows better than I do what I'm feeling!

Even though I am searingly honest with him, it is Ron who is in denial.

My family doesn't care for his know-it-all manner. Generally, Mom welcomes all kinds of people, but Ron has made a poor impression. Lita isn't too thrilled with him, either.

I know he behaves like an ass, but I cling to him to keep my crazy thoughts at bay.

A phone call from my friend, Connie, an Al-Anon friend, changes this situation entirely.

"I don't know if you'll be mad at me for telling you this," she says hesitantly. "But Ron is married."

"But he lives alone in his apartment. I've been there, and there's no sign of anyone else."

"But he IS married. He and his wife were married for only a few months when he left her."

"Oh my God!"

"And get this! His wife attends the same Al-Anon meeting we do."

"NO!"

"You see, I put two and two together," continues Connie. "With Corrine talking about her husband and you talking about Ron—he sounds exactly like the same guy! I thought I better warn you before Corrine figures this out!"

I thank Connie fervently.

The next time Ron comes to pick me up, I confront him. He confessed sheepishly that, yes, he was married. "But my relationship with you is so much better than it was with Corrine!" He looked at me pleadingly.

"You lied to me. You told me you were divorced!"

"I wasn't lying. I am divorced—from my first wife!"

"But you left out the fact that you're married."

"Well, I figured if I told you I'm married, you wouldn't go out with me!"

"You're right. I wouldn't have!" And so, it's goodbye to Ron!"

It seems I'm overdue for a major self-examination. *Now, I realize I am not in any mental and emotional shape to be in a relationship with a man.* So, I resolve not to date at all until I'm feeling better.

Wailing

So many times, I feel misunderstood
When little people try to make me feel no good
And then I feel just like a little child
Alone and lost, abandoned, scared and wild
CHORUS: (Wailing) ah-ah, ah-ah ah-ah,
ah-ha, ah-ah ah-ah

Lord, must I always feel this pain
Is there truly good that can be gained
Will the sunshine follow on the rain
Lord, I gotta know

So many times I've been knocked to the ground
Nobody near to help me come around
and then I feel just like a little child
alone and lost abandoned, scared and wild
CHORUS: wailing

Lord, why do you 'llow the things you do?
Is what they say about love true?
If you give will it all come back to you?
Lord, I gotta know.

So many times it feels like You're don't care
I call your name, can't find you anywhere
and then I feel just like a little child
alone and lost, abandoned, scared and wild

CHORUS: more wailing

Where are You, God? Where are You?

23

Looking for Help in all the Wrong Places

y first port of call was with a New Age minister. Lydia was an older lady, very popular in her small church. Her teachings focused on the use of denials and affirmations. We were to repeatedly say to ourselves that a negative situation has no power over us, knowing that an affirmation we constantly repeat will draw the positive experiences we want to manifest in our lives.

"Never talk about this to anyone again," she advised me. "Just keep repeating that your past has no power over you." Then, she gave me an affirmation to use: "With God's help, I'm feeling stronger and happier each day."

I knew right away that this approach wouldn't work for me. It would like saying, "This ticking time bomb will not explode." No way would such a denial prevent an explosion! I needed to look for help elsewhere.

I could have gone to see a psychiatrist; however, I didn't trust members of that profession. Also, on my Crisis Line shifts, some callers would complain that they were addicted to the drug of the day—Valium. So, I decided instead to see a counsellor. What can I say? She was very nice and a good listener. She empathized with me. She told me I was very brave to break off with Paul and that now I was on the yellow brick road to healing, but it would take some time. We had several fruitless sessions.

My next counsellor was a nice guy and also a good listener. He empathized with me and told me I was very brave to break off with Paul. Healing would take some time, but I'd made a good start. More fruitless sessions!

I liked both counsellors, but talking-head therapy didn't work. Something was missing, but I didn't know what it could be.

In the meantime, I clung to my Al-Anon meetings. While Al-Anon couldn't resolve my heavy-duty issues, I had the support and encouragement of honest warm-hearted people.

God, what was I going to do? Was there nothing that could help me? Finally, desperation led me to throw myself at the mercy of the Mental Health Clinic. If they admitted me into the mental hospital, then so be it.

A tall, imposing woman led me into her office. "Now tell me what brings you here," she said brusquely.

I poured out my deepest fears about my compulsive thoughts and impulses. "I'm so scared I might hurt someone or injure myself, but I can't stop these thoughts. They keep coming back! Do I need to be admitted?"

She leaned toward me, fixing me with a hard stare.

"Many people come here wanting us to admit them, but the truth is that they use mental illness as a screen to avoid their responsibilities!"

Huh? I stared at her. How could she say that? She didn't even know me! Wasn't I being responsible, coming here for help? The woman was an iceberg.

"If you stab yourself in the eye, you will be blind in that eye. If you kill someone, you will go to jail," she stated. "Now, is there anything else?"

I was wrong. At least icebergs melt. She was a stone-cold, unyielding granite monolith.

"No," I faltered.

"Good. I do not think you need to see me again."

And just like that, dismissed, with no suggestions of where I might find alternative help! Once again, there was just Me, Myself, and I. The three of me were running out of options. "Alone Again (Naturally)," Gilbert O'Sullivan.

I sat down on a bench outside the office and stared down the long road with its endless array of robotic cars swishing by. I stared at the leaden sky. My spirit wanted to lay down and die. I just wanted to die. In my mind, I was dead already, but, out of habit, my body slowly rose from the bench and slogged on through the wet rain-sodden street.

"What kept you from attempting suicide?" a friend asked me years later.

Three things. The first was thanks to the Catholic Church; if you committed suicide, you'd go straight to hell to languish in torment forever and ever. I hadn't set foot in the church for several years, but that old teaching still had the power to scare me.

The second reason also made me hesitate. I'd been reading several books written by psychics, and some claimed that suicides quickly boomeranged back to earth to live out a new life with similar issues. This cycle would go on and on, continuing until the souls learned not to take their own lives. Lord knows how long that would take!

Also, I didn't wish to die in a state of hopelessness. What kept me going? Sheer stubbornness. I determined that someday, somehow, I would find the help I needed.

☙

Shortly after my disastrous visit to the mental health centre, an incident shook me.

One sunny day, on my way home from some downtown shopping, I came face-to-face with Paul and a pretty dark-haired young woman—holding hands, the two of them looking radiant. I knew who she was. I just knew.

How did I know this woman was Linda? During the dinosaur era, long before the Internet was hatched, there was The City Directory. This Directory listed residents living at a certain address. When I checked several years later, sure enough, Paul and Linda were listed at the same address for seven years.

Sickened, I was silent, passing them with eyes straight ahead like a blinkered horse. Peripherally, I saw Paul give a start and murmur something to Linda, who didn't know me by sight.

Back at home, I wondered at the turbulence of my emotions. Certainly, I had no desire to return to this relationship, yet how dare he be so effing happy while I'm drowning, struggling for my very life, still trying to resist the pull of my treacherous vortex. It wasn't fair! And was I so easily replaceable?

I never hated anyone with such intensity, not even my poor father on his worst drunken days.

I had to get away. I had to get away from all the sad, bad memories and the daily grind of office work where I put on a happy face. I had to get away from everything, and for sure I didn't want to bump into the happy couple again!

As it happened, I had a feasible plan. I would return to university and complete a Bachelor of Arts degree—away from my hometown.

One day, sorting through various university calendars, I found it! Nestled in the heart of the West Kootenays was the small town of Nelson, BC. Nestled in the heart of Nelson was a small university located on a pleasant hillside.

This campus was it! Eagerly, I signed up for English, theatre, and philosophy courses, and they accepted me as a mature student.

Over the next year, I saved enough money to pay for my classes. As for the rest of the expenses, I would get by with student loans.

To that end, I focussed intently on my job. I was still employed, having "shaped up." Due to my improvement, my boss didn't tell me to "ship out!" Instead, he gave me a good appraisal.

That year was a quiet one. Mostly I just hung out with my family and friends and worked toward my goal. I was still not mentally well, but now I had something to look forward to; hope gave me wings.

24

AHA! PHOBIC NEURRROTIC!

N otre Dame was at one time a Catholic university but now had become secular.

Approximately 500 students from the outlying areas attended classes held in the main building. The campus also featured a gymnasium, a cafeteria, and a small library. A tiny chapel sat in the middle. Another building housed the junior dorms for women, where I lived for my first year. Later I moved into a larger complex, which took up the third and fourth floors for the men's and senior women's dorms. The first two floors were dedicated to the town's only live theatre. Finally, of course, was the most important building of all, a small SUB (Students' Union Building) where guys and girls could hang out.

My first year at NDU was platinum. Everything I wanted, everything I needed, was contained within the cozy cocoon of the campus.

Friends, dates, parties, classes, profs, food, dances, international students, acting, singing, plays, musicals, sub sandwiches at the SUB, term papers, cramming, exams, library, sledding on stolen cafeteria trays, raiding the boys' dorm, pranks, bursaries, 10 pm Chinese feasts cooked by Chinese students—I had it all.

I wasn't the most serious student. As long as I maintained a B average, which I did, along with an occasional B+, I felt free to live life to the max!

At an event that welcomed new students, I met the "gang" I would hang out with, including four men and three women. Gloria and Lorraine, mature students like myself, were studying for a teaching certificate; Nora's ambition was to become a social worker.

Two of the guys, Tony and Mark, were headed for the priesthood (one Catholic and the other Anglican). Bob, Mark's younger brother, worked with lighting in the theatre. Hamzah hailed from Indonesia.

Now here was the opportunity I'd missed growing up; seeing that men could be friends. It felt good to drop my former negative labels of them as potential letches or male chauvinist pigs!

On several occasions, Hamzah confided his romantic woes to me. One night, he made me a beautiful card with the words, "You are the moonlight in my dark endless night."

At a party one night, I met Arif, a student from Iran. We dated for a few months, although it was never a serious relationship. Our cultural differences were too extensive, resulting in several clashes. Mostly we just had fun.

Sometime later, I went for a couple of outings with Leo, Gloria's brother, who was just visiting.

I didn't need drugs or alcohol to get high. Being wary of any mind-altering substances, the most I succumbed to was the occasional wine flip (7 Up mixed with red wine).

I loved my acting courses and was delighted to be cast in two plays, one of them a musical. As NDU held the town's only live theatre, they also cast people from town, outside the university, creating a diverse social milieu. I no longer had to "put on a happy face"; I *was* a happy face! But then came summer. Bummer summer!

All my friends had left for their respective hometowns, leaving me alone on a near-empty campus.

Not wanting to live on my own in a deserted dorm, I rented a small furnished one-bedroom apartment in a charming older house on a pleasant tree-lined street. I had applied for a job in the English department. My task was to interview women writers living in the Kootenay area. Most of these women met at the Women's Centre in Nelson, so I was off to a good start. While I enjoyed learning about these dynamic women, I had too much time on my hands as it was a part-time job.

We're BAA-ACK! All your bogeymen! Thought you could get rid of us, did you? Thought you could crowd us out with your dizzy, busy-busy-busyness? Ha! We've been waiting for you, honey! You'll never get rid of us! NEVER, NEVER, NEVER EVER! BWA-HA-HA-HA-HA!

Yup! Everything I had suppressed during my wonderful, colourful year was back in full force.

WAAH! What could I do? Long uphill and downhill walks to explore the beautiful local scenery failed to distract me, as did shopping on downtown Baker Street. The tiny library had a limited selection of books, and the local movie theatre featured films I'd seen several years earlier. With no close friends and no family to distract me, my fearful thoughts held sway.

It's got to be my guilt causing this craziness. I wonder; I do come from a Roman Catholic background. If I rejoined the church and confessed to a priest, would that help? Would I feel absolved and forgiven?

So that's what I did. Father Osmond was a nice young guy. I did not kneel in a confessional but was seated in the parlour of the priest's house. I poured out my sins and got absolution and a warm welcome back into the arms of Mother Church.

Did that help? Sitting at mass on Sundays, I realized that I couldn't, in all honesty, say the Apostles' Creed. So many of my old beliefs had dropped away. Once again, my thoughts frightened me.

Maybe I wasn't trying hard enough.

Then I heard from one lady about a small charismatic group that met once a week. The Charismatics are what I call Super Catholics; they strictly adhere to the church's teachings and they're as rigorous in their Bible reading as any protestant fundamentalist. They meet to commune with the Holy Spirit, who inspires them to give messages that they or others may need to hear.

WOW! That was it. Maybe this group was my way back to sanity.

A warm Tuesday evening found me in a small lounge with twelve people. There was also a priest. The service opened with a few prayers and some Bible readings, followed by a long silence. Then, whenever someone felt moved by the Spirit, they could get up to speak. At length, one woman earnestly told us that women should not speak at services, according to the apostle Paul. *So, what was she doing speaking at a service?* A couple of other people spoke after her, mainly quoting teachings from the Bible.

Finally, when the meeting ended, a man approached the priest. "Father, would you please say a prayer to protect us from the Devil?"

Everyone bowed heads as the priest uttered a prayer.

Protection from the Devil? What was the Devil doing at a charismatic meeting? I shuddered.

Overall, I was unimpressed.

The second meeting was much like the first. The same woman got up again to inform us that women should let men be the head of the house because the apostle Paul said so. *Jesus, I wish she would follow her earlier message to keep her mouth shut! What century does she live in, anyway?* Once again, the meeting ended with a prayer of protection from the Devil.

I did speak briefly with one fellow. I'll never forget him!

"Whenever I get a headache, I pray to God. 'Lord, if the Devil caused this headache, please heal me at once. If not, I'll endure it.' And do you know what?"

"What?"

"Most of the time, it vanishes! Just like that!"

"Why would the Devil give you headaches?"

"Because he's always on the lookout to harass Christians especially close to God," he smiled triumphantly, his eyes glowing.

God, this guy is more bonkers than I am! Well! I certainly don't want to attend any services that focus on the Devil!

Thus ended my brief affair with this charismatic group. Shortly afterwards, I parted ways with the Catholic Church altogether.

Unfortunately, that man with the glowing eyes unveiled an old childhood fear of mine.

"Mama! Mama! I dreamed that the Devil came to take me away! Is he going to take me away? Mama, I'm scared!"

"No, no, dear child, I won't let him take you away. I won't let him!"

The idea sprouted like an invasive plant sending its evil tendrils to entangle my already over-taxed mind. God had spurned my pitiful attempts at repentance, leaving me totally at the mercy of you-know-who! The Devil planted the violent thoughts and urges I experienced earlier. Any time now, he would come to possess me!

Rationally, I knew it didn't make sense, but what good is rationalism at 11 pm, 3 am, and 5 am? Sleep eluded me as I dwelled in a whole miasma of terror. I'd sit shivering through the night. Sadly, my mommy wasn't there to chase the nightmares away.

One evening, I couldn't stand it anymore. I couldn't bear to spend one more night on my own. Desperately, I fled to the local hospital, a mile away, and sobbed my heart out at the nurses' desk.

The kind nurse tried to make sense of my rambling. "We have a psychiatrist on duty. I'll send him to talk to you."

The shrink was in his late fifties and had a Germanic accent. I'll call him Dr. Freudlich. After listening to me, he pounced. "AHA! PHOBIC NEURRROTIC!" He rolled his Rs as magnificently as any Scotsman!

That was it? That was my diagnosis? Phobic Neurotic is "psychiatrese" for Scaredy-Cat. I could have told him that! However, I was grateful, oh so grateful, to the good doctor when he announced that they would admit me for five days for further assessment.

This hospital didn't have a ward for mental illness patients, only for those admitted for assessment. If they showed signs of a severe mental condition, they would transfer them to Essondale Asylum at Riverview Hospital, a heavy-duty mental institute in Coquitlam.

The ward featured a pleasant lounge with couches and armchairs and a table and chairs. A few bedrooms were off to the side. I honestly can't remember whether I shared a room or was on my own. When the nurse gave me a sleeping pill, I thought I'd died and gone to heaven. I slept like a baby.

I woke up refreshed and happy, happy, happy. Happy to be looked after. Happy not to be alone. I was so happy that I positively glowed.

Another patient, a woman, asked me curiously, "What are *you* doing here?"

My other medication was the dreaded Valium. Well, it did calm me down.

In the ward, they provided a supply of paper, coloured pencils, felt pens, and crayons. I decided to do some art therapy. I felt furious at the Catholic Church for implanting the idea of the Devil and eternal Hell in the vulnerable mind of a seven-year-old child and scaring the daylights out of my 26-year-old self!

I drew an evil-looking bishop who was holding the wings of a little green figure chained to his wrist. The little green person wanted to fly toward the light. A mean priest was watching. I included these words.

Thou shalt not think!
Thou shalt not feel!
Thou shall not be free!

At that point, who should walk in unexpectedly, but an elderly priest. "Well, what have we here?" he cheerfully said after he had greeted me. "May I see?"

Oh Jeez! I knew this was going to be so awkward. I uncovered my handiwork.

His eyes widened. He backed away and sputtered, "Tear that up! Throw it away!" He shot out of the room as if

I was Satan himself! I was delighted! Now it was my turn to scare the hell out of a priest. Maybe it was his karma!

When the five days were up, I was sent home with a bottle of Valium and instructions to make an appointment with Dr. Freudlich one month later. Unfortunately, the Valium made me pretty dopey, and I stumbled and almost fell downhill on my way back to my residence. I was so scared I'd become addicted to this drug that I flushed it down the toilet after a few days.

Mom came to stay for a week, cooking tasty meals and rearranging my furniture as a mother's prerogative. We had long heart-to-heart talks, and she drew me some sketches of the local scenery and my cozy apartment. Then, all too soon, our time together drew to an end, and once again, I was on my own.

25

I Begin to Heal

*W*hat am I going to do now? Will I ever overcome this thing? Will I ever find the help I need? Maybe I should not have flushed the Valium down the toilet. Feeling so anxious. One more month before classes start again. What am I going to do?

What happened next was thanks to Martha at the Women's Centre. "Did you know there's going to be a week-long Gestalt therapy workshop in the Slocan Valley?" She knew about my recent crash.

"I don't know if I can afford it," I replied.

"Oh, but you can! It's run by a woman called Bethel who wants to help people who *don't* have a lot of money. Most people in the Slocan Valley don't have much. It's $30.00 for the week or $30.00 worth of groceries!"

"Seriously? Is she any good?"

"Many people from around here have gone to her, and they love her! Mind you, the conditions are pretty rustic. You'd have to sleep in a tent."

"But I don't have a tent!"

"People bring their own, but a few are on the property."

"But I don't have a car!"

"One of the women here is going. I'm sure she'd give you a ride."

That is how I found myself in the middle of a forest one week later in a large tent that I was to share with four other people—two couples. Oh my God, what had I done? What if this whole business turned weird and freaky? I'd have no means of escape!

The tent where my "roomies" and I would sleep was the hub of our soul-baring adventures. Having settled myself on a large cushion, I looked around at the men and women. Most were in their twenties and thirties. About a dozen of us were sitting in a circle around a gym mat, a huge pillow, and a steel pipe. Apprehensively, I wondered what was going to be done with that pipe.

Bethel was a trim older woman with white hair, dressed in a long denim skirt and a tank top. She welcomed us all and told us about Gestalt therapy.

"Fritz Perls and his wife Laura developed Gestalt therapy as an alternative to traditional psychoanalysis. It focuses on the present rather than delving into the past," she explained. "The focus is on understanding what is taking place in your life now and taking personal responsibility rather than placing blame."

I didn't fully get her explanation but was sure I'd find out. I was going to play the role of a cautious observer.

A man called Ted was the first to go up. He was angry with his father and effectively expressed that anger by repeatedly striking the pillow with the pipe. I watched as several other people took their turns. Soon, my apprehension turned into anticipation. I could hardly wait!

When it was my turn, I was more than ready. I was going to beat the shit out of Paul! Upon explaining my issue to the group, I picked up the pipe and started to pound on the pillow.

"YOU BASTARD!" THWACK, THWACK!

"YOU ASSHOLE!" THWACK!

Bethel stopped me in mid-thwack. "No name-calling! It's important to use 'I' statements and to take responsibility for your feelings. You can say something like, 'you put me down in front of others, and I felt embarrassed. I hate you for it!'"

I nodded and turned to address the cushion (Paul).

"YOU WERE MY COUNSELLOR AND TOOK ADVANTAGE OF MY VULNERABILITY, AND I HATE YOU FOR IT!"

All through the week, I poured out my rage. Between me and the others in my group, I honestly don't know how that pillow managed to survive!

At one point, I watched as one guy went through a particularly gruelling session. When he finished, Bethel instructed him to drink some water, go outside, and throw up. I was astounded! Bethel explained to the rest of us that this strategy was a way to deal with intense pressure. My God, was *that* what I had been doing?

I became friendly with Jenny, who, as a popular song of that time, was "torn between two lovers." Her parents brought her up going to a church that stressed positive affirmations. Her family did not tolerate "negative feelings," such as anger or sadness, in that household. It didn't do her much good.

There was friction between two members of our group. Ted couldn't stand Irene and kept sniping at her, and Irene, in turn, took verbal swipes at him. Finally, after a few days, Bethel called them both to the mat to role play. Back and forth they went, seemingly getting nowhere.

"Okay," Bethel interrupted. "Ted, you be Irene, and Irene, you be Ted."

Back and forth, the couple went, again without much of a result.

Bethel interrupted once more. "Ted, what gets you the most about Irene?"

"Her smile," he answered. "It's so smug and superior. It's like she feels she's above the rest of us."

"Ted, would you please imitate that smile."

Ted stretched his lips into a tooth-baring grimace.

"How are you feeling when you do that?" asked Bethel.

Ted paused. "I feel—insecure." He sounded surprised.

"Irene, is that how you feel?"

Irene nodded.

"Oh," said Ted in a small voice.

The battle came to an end. Ted based his antipathy toward Irene on her smile. The role-playing impressed me very much. Later, I watched as a lesbian couple resolved some of their issues using the same technique.

Going back to church had intensified my old fear of going to Hell. So, with the support of Bethel and the group, I gave Father Hell and the nasty nun who condemned my parents a few good healthy THWACKS on that day!

Overall, this workshop was a very intense but cleansing experience. Miracle of miracles, all thoughts of hurting myself or others had vanished, and all fears of being possessed by the devil! I couldn't believe it. *Are these urges going to come back?* I wondered. They never did. The Gestalt therapy had been as good as an exorcism!

Now I understood why my previous counselling had failed. We humans are not just talking heads. We inhabit our whole body. Bethel's workshop had offered a physical release.

My next task was to rebuild myself. I hoped to return to being the girl with the shining dreams and high ideals, but that was not to be, at least not the same way. Instead, I needed to find out who I was now after my harrowing experience. It was an uphill task and would take more time and therapy.

One thing I was sure of, however, was that I had begun to heal.

26

Moving On

If my first year at NDU was platinum, the last year was silver, the colour of a waning moon. It was still a great year, but news that the university would cease to function as Notre Dame University in 1976 put a damper on students' spirits. As for me, I stayed behind to complete the courses I needed to graduate. Luckily, I met another mature student, a lovely girl from Trinidad. We decided to move from the dorm to the Marianne Apartments for senior students just a couple of blocks away from the campus. Carol and I became quite close and spent hours talking about everything under the sun. We also got to know some young married students living in the building and had visits from our friends. So, there was still a good social life. I got a part in another play as well as a temporary part-time job as the theatre manager.

Later that year, my friends and I took part in a protest at the closure of our Alma Mater, walking down Baker Street and chanting, "HELL NO! WE WON'T GO!" Back home, Mom was astounded to see me on the TV news!

In June of that year, our graduation was held in the town's movie theatre. As a Scottish piper was leading us into the building, I started crying, and, for the life of me, I couldn't stop! Oh dear, where was the Kleenex when I needed it? I had so loved my courses, all my new friends, and the terrific experiences I'd had. I just managed to stop sniffling in time to walk up the steps to the stage and collect my diploma—a BA in Theatre and English! Mom was there, staying for a week with Carol and me. She was also my prom date.

Back in my hometown, a friend's mother wasted no time giving me her opinion of my BA. "Theatre and English? That's only good for standing in line at the employment office." In a way, she was right, but it did net me a couple of interesting temporary jobs as a writer-researcher tailor-made for grads. In any case, my typing skills never left me without work for too long. She didn't know that I'd be leaving town soon to seek fame and fortune.

Where in Canada would a wannabe singer-songwriter go? To Toronto, of course! I knew only one person living there; otherwise, I don't know if I would have had the courage to go. I decided to travel by train to see the sights in my vast country. The Rockies were my favourite by far.

In Toronto, the oppressive June heat seemed to suck the life out of me, and the size of the city was overwhelming. The tall buildings seemed to stretch to infinity. I remember looking for a particular address, and when I arrived, it wasn't the correct building. "You probably want 23309 East; this is 23309 West," explained a woman at the counter. I was flabbergasted! Can you imagine a street so long that they divide it into East and West?

Gazing at the endless cars whizzing by and side-stepping a few odd characters I passed on the street, I thought, *my goodness, if anything happens to me, no one will miss me for days!*

The dumpy furnished bachelor suite I found was situated only a few blocks from Yorkville. Formerly a hippy hangout, this area boasted reputable shops and restaurants. I discovered an eatery that advertised a free meal to all who took part in their open-mic jams. Gathering all my courage, I hit the stage, ready to take the audience by storm with my best three songs. Sadly, no producer jumped up from a table to sign me up for a recording company. No one was even listening. People were more interested in eating and chatting. However, I did get a good dinner out of the deal. I returned the following week with the same result. Disappointed, I walked home with my tail between my legs—that is, if I had a tail. You know what I mean!

Next up was a song-writing contest put on by a producer who at one time coached Gordon Lightfoot. The prize was a free record production. Contestants were encouraged to bring several of their best songs.

No, I didn't win. This producer told me, "Beth, you're an excellent lyricist, but your songs are non-commercial. And they need to fit into three minutes of airtime."

One of my songs had the word "damn" in it, which wasn't acceptable either.

However, he did offer to coach me on one of my songs that had commercial possibilities—for a fee, of course. Later, if I wanted to record this song, that would also come out of my pocketbook.

I went for a few sessions but decided that this path was not for me. I felt the steel strings of my new guitar digging into my fingers. If I practiced enough, eventually, they would get calluses. Also, I needed to learn more than the sixteen chords I already knew. Some of these new chords required complex fingering. Finally, I grew frustrated with the practice and gave up on my lessons.

Shortly afterwards, I found work as a secretary for Mr. Lemon-Face. I called him that because his sour expression made me think that he constantly sucked on lemons! I never saw him smile. However, I made a couple of new friends in that office, and we hung out a lot.

There were many things that I loved about Toronto. I loved the ethnic neighbourhoods. A short subway ride would take me to a different clime and culture. I moved to better digs in the Polish-Russian area in Bloor West Village, a one-bedroom apartment only a few blocks from a Polish deli!! I loved Folkfest—for which they gave me a passport to visit the many "countries" located in various areas of the city. I loved Honest Ed's, the variety store with the goofy signs. ("How is Honest Ed like an obstetrician? He always delivers.") Ed Mirvish was also the founder of a theatre and a restaurant that he launched, each with his unique over-the-top style. The Lake Ontario shoreline was the site of many events. The Toronto Zoo was the best I ever visited; you could only view the animals from a train. They had ample room to rove and live as natural a life as possible. There was always something interesting going on in this city.

I fell in love for the second time. Jason was a graduate of MIT and worked as a software consultant. He was single and just a year older than me. We first met at a Quaker meeting house during their coffee hour after the service. Jason invited me out for coffee, where we wound up talking for four hours. Later, we enjoyed many fun-filled dates. We were together for a year.

This relationship did not go smoothly. Jason was gun-shy of matrimony.

"Marriage!" he exclaimed. "A house with a mortgage, two kids, and a dog! Thanks, but no thanks!"

"How about a condo, no kids, and a cat?" I offered hopefully. I was serious, having made up my mind that he was "The One." He didn't bite.

The more I clung to him, the less he wanted to see me. Eventually, we broke up. However, for my 30th birthday, Jason treated me to supper at the revolving restaurant atop the CN Tower.

When Mr. Lemon-Face threatened to fire me, I felt it was time to leave that job. I missed my family and close friends back home, so I returned to start the next chapter in my life.

I was so happy to reconnect with my family and friends back in my hometown. It didn't take me long to find employment as a library clerk. I also found a one-bedroom apartment in a pleasant neighbourhood. Lita lived next door. A friend also lived in the same building. I had enough money this time to buy my own furniture and decorate the rooms to my taste. I was pleased with the result.

27

My True Love and I

My life was going smoothly, yet I yearned for long-lasting love, not simply a romance. I wanted to marry. Missing was a "Who." However, it seemed that all the "good guys" were taken, and I was not into the bar scene. I asked God to help me. This time I did not make a list. "God, please help me find someone who is right for me."

Dan and I met through a dating service. The lady who ran the service interviewed prospective members in their own homes. She explained that she did this to weed out weirdos and married men on the make. I admired how she arranged the matches. Simone would phone me first. She'd say, "I have someone you might be interested in." She'd give me the name and details of the prospective boyfriend, then ask, "Shall I give him your phone number?" It was up to me to say "yes" or "no"!

Dan was my third prospect. We went to a quiet up-scale bar where we could hear ourselves talk. I found that Dan had quite a sense of humour, was into reading Omni magazine (which I also enjoyed) and told some interesting stories about gold-panning with a friend. He was also a talented artist. When he was in grade four, there was a city-wide contest for the best child's painting. The prize was free art lessons given by the local art gallery. Dan won. Unfortunately, his dad told Dan in no uncertain terms that he had to get a regular job "or else!" once he graduated from high school, so Dan managed to get steady employment with the provincial government where he worked for the next 37 years. I was happy to learn that he was not a big drinker and not into drugs. Like me, he'd never been married. He pursued his interest in art through various night courses.

We visited museums and the art gallery. We explored various beaches. Dan cooked delicious meals—Chinese dinners, Greek meatballs with pasta, Pommes Parisienne (a fancy name for potatoes) with juicy steaks. He tastefully decorated his apartment with good furniture and his artwork. I treated Dan to some of my home cooking. When I asked him what he thought about my culinary attempts, he answered, "Nothing to write home about!" I laughed because it was true.

Several months later, Dan asked me to marry him. It was Christmas morning. I accepted. Together, we chose a beautiful Victorian-style citrine quartz ring with three small diamonds. It would be almost two years before we married, which gave us ample time to meet each other's families and get to know each other better.

Did I tell Dan about Paul and Jason? As it happened, we each drew a veil over our past loves. We never asked each other about our earlier relationships, preferring to focus on our present and future together.

Dan was not a churchgoer, so he empathized with my conflict regarding certain Catholic Church and fundamentalist Christian teachings. However, during our engagement, I attended a Unity Church service. Unity is Christian in its orientation, emphasizing one's positive relationship with a loving God. The people were friendly and welcoming. I felt that I had found a spiritual home and attended for a good many years.

We did have one kerfuffle before our wedding.

One day, Dan looked at me and said, "Whatever you do after we get married, don't get fat."

Those were fighting words! I told him frankly about my struggles with overeating and bulimia and that he would have to accept me however much I weighed. Yes, I did gain weight—35 pounds—during our marriage, and Dan wasn't too happy about the extra pounds; however, he never reproached me for it. I did join Weight Watchers several times, losing and gaining the same 15 pounds repeatedly.

We also discussed the issue of having children. I had no desire to become a parent in my thirties. Being the oldest child in my family, I never romanticized parenthood nor the sacrifices this would require. Instead, I planted a magnet on my fridge that said, "If I want to hear the pitter-patter of little feet, I'll put shoes on my cat!" Dan was okay with this decision; we would be free to pursue our creative interests. We had cats instead, one of each—a boy and a girl!

Our wedding took place on a beautiful September day. I had my hair French-braided with creamy silk flowers and wore an afternoon-length cream-coloured dress. My brother Ray walked me down the aisle, and Lita was my matron of honour, pretty in peach. (By this time, she had married her high school sweetheart.) We were married in the Unity church witnessed by thirty of our closest friends and family. Afterwards, we celebrated at the small house that Dan and I had rented a few months earlier. The catered food was delicious, and all of us danced and had a great time. Then, Dan and I spent our honeymoon at a beach resort.

Shortly after we were married, my bulimic episodes decreased to once a week. I was loved; I was cared for. I felt secure in my relationship with Dan.

We were each creative and very supportive of each other. When my Unity church was having an arts and crafts day, I encouraged Dan to bring some of his artwork. One of our church members was the owner of an art gallery. The rest, as they say, is history; not that Dan shot overnight to fame, but he had several shows of his work and met fellow artists. He sold two of his pictures, one for $800.00 and another for $1,000.00. In turn, Dan would listen patiently to my writing attempts and give me feedback. Whenever I coordinated yearly talent shows at another church I later attended, Dan helped, setting out chairs, taking money, and once, building a TV set for a skit. He had my back, and I had his.

During those years, I practised stand-up comedy using my original material and sang some of my songs at those talent shows, so my BA in Theatre and English wasn't a total waste!

With twinkling eyes, Dan once described how he saw our marriage. "Beth is like a kite that takes off into the air, but when she drifts too high, I have to reel her in," he said, and so he did, but always gently. We were together for 31 years.

28

"BIO"

S adly, my bulimic tendencies continued. By this time, some articles had come out in magazines about bulimia. I was astounded to learn that many young women—especially college students—deliberately used this method to lose weight. However, knowing the name of my disease didn't help me overcome it. This nasty habit resulted in gastritis and an acidic throat from the bile.

I attended Overeaters Anonymous for a few years, "talked the talk," and took my turn to chair meetings. I quit when I realized that I *wasn't* "walking the walk." However, I did make a couple of really good friends with whom I stayed in touch.

My next attempt was to sign up for a ten-week session for women trying to recover from bulimia. The counsellor, Jean, was a large, overweight woman who confessed to our small group that she was still trying to control her overeating. Mostly, the eight of us talked about what triggered us and our progress from week to week. She gave us sheets of paper to write a food plan for the next seven days. Certainly, this list wouldn't include our trigger foods.

One evening, we were astounded to see Jean arrive with staples in her ear lobes!

"This is supposed to help stop my cravings," she explained.

Oh.

I empathized; she and I belonged to the same tribe. When the course came to an end, I wondered whether I should recommend Overeaters Anonymous to Jean. I wish I had now. After all, that program *has* worked for many. I did not sign up for a second session.

Briefly, I thought about getting my ears stapled, but I didn't know if my stapler was the right kind for doing the job myself!

Life is always throwing us curve balls. I'd been fired from a well-paying job; it was a poor decision to apply for the higher position that I liked less, but Dan and I were talking about buying a house, and the extra money would come in handy. I had no idea what to say to prospective employers. "I left my last job because they promoted me to the level of my incompetence, and they terminated me." That's exactly how I felt—terminated! My self-confidence was in tatters. Also, I still found it difficult to assert myself.

I decided that I needed more therapy. However, being on unemployment insurance meant less money coming in, so where would I go? As luck would have it, I heard about a nurse well on her way to becoming a licensed therapist in Bioenergetics, a therapy developed by Dr. Alexander Lowen, a descendant of Wilhelm Reich. She was accepting clients with whom to do her practice. If she ran into any problems, she could discuss them with a supervisor. She would charge only $25.00 an hour. I jumped on it.

What is "bio"? Our body constructs defenses to guard against trauma. Along with this comes stored, unexpressed emotions which continue to be felt as emotional and psychic tension. The practice is based on releasing the repressed physical and psychic energy through various psychological and physical exercises. I spent two productive years with Amey, a very understanding and compassionate woman. This therapy turned out to be *a major milestone* in my healing!

Amey had reserved a room in her home to conduct the sessions, with a wooden carpenter's "horse" and a gym mat on the carpeted floor. The first time, I glanced around nervously, particularly at the sawhorse. What was that for?

She started me off simply with a basic grounding exercise. I was to stand, legs apart at the hip with bent knees, feet facing forward. My lower legs were to do the work of supporting me. This position was harder to do than it sounds, as I was accustomed to locking my knees. However, as I did this position, I could feel the strength in my lower legs, and I started to vibrate. Then I was to slowly curl myself forward, let my arms hang loosely, and touch the floor with my hands, head hanging down. Amey encouraged me to make a continual "aah" sound. Well, like Elvis said, "There was a whole lot of shakin' going on." That was the point of the exercise.

Next, there was the sawhorse. I was to bend over backwards, hands over my head, with the "horse" supporting my back, and make the "ah" sound. Amey explained that bending back over the sawhorse (it was cushioned), allowed my chest to expand, breathing to deepen, and more tender sounds to emerge.

The third exercise was on the gym mat—the temper tantrum. I was to kick my legs as strongly as I could and yell, "NO NO NO NO!" I was disappointed that we wouldn't be doing the pillow-pounding thing, but Amey said that I needed to develop strength in my legs; they weren't strong, making me physically and emotionally susceptible to being pushed around.

These were the exercises we focused on over the next two years.

What sense was there in that? It makes a whole lot of sense. Since the idea is that we store our unexpressed emotions in our bodies, the exercises are designed to let these emotions out without a lot of verbiage.

For example, at one appointment, Amey asked how I was feeling. I told her that my mood was neutral—neither happy nor sad. After going through the grounding exercise, she directed me to the sawhorse. Back I bent, vocalizing "aah aah aah aah." Suddenly, my "aahs" grew louder, gradually turning into wails, and I cried, and I cried, and I cried. I cried as if my heart would break. Sometimes an image would come with that, sometimes not. Well, I sure surprised myself that day!

If an image arose with the emotion, Amey and I would talk about that. If not, then it was just good to get that feeling out of my body.

One time, Dan and I had a fight. Close to my birthday, we were wandering through a shop in Chinatown. There, I saw a beautiful statue of Kwan Yin, the Chinese goddess of Mercy, arrayed in a dazzling white robe. I immediately knew what I wanted as a birthday gift. I pointed her out to Dan.

The following week, I eagerly unwrapped the gift box—only to pull out a Kwan Yin statue arrayed in a green robe.

"But I wanted the white one!"

Dan pointed out that the glazing on the green one was artistically superior. Ergo this was the better choice. He seemed quite pleased with himself.

"But I liked the white one the best!" I wailed.

"But the green one has better glaze," he insisted.

"I wanted the **WHITE ONE!***" I countered.

"But the green one is artistically superior," he countered. And on and on, we continued with this stupid argument.

WAH! The next day, I hurried to Chinatown, turned into the store, and purchased the white Kwan Yin.

Now we had two Kwan Yins eyeing each other from opposite corners of the living room like boxing opponents.

When I told Amey this story, she exclaimed, "WHAT? You didn't take back the green one to make an exchange?"

I nodded sheepishly, aware that, once again, I had copped out.

"GET ON THAT MAT!" stated Amey. We both burst out laughing.

Of course, this situation brought to mind the unwanted gift that Paul had given me. What is it with men? I did feel that I'd made some progress, though. I hadn't said anything to Paul; I pretended that his choice was what I wanted. At least I verbalized my displeasure to Dan, and I did buy myself the gift I preferred!

Well into the second year, I had a waking vision. In my mind's eye, I kept seeing a cougar up in a tree. I was down below, looking up at her, unafraid. Gracefully, she leaped from the tree and padded toward me. I knew I was to follow her. She led me to a river, the beginning of her boundary. She led me around her land, silently instructing me that I also had borders that I should defend. Cougar wasn't interested in acquiring the territory of other animals, only keeping what was hers. She looked upon me as a half-grown cub who needed some teaching.

When I told Amey about my visionary encounter, she instructed me to lay down on the mat and *be* the cougar.

I growled and clawed the air with my fingers. I felt powerful, strong, and serene. Something in my psyche had shifted.

What came out of my two years of "bio" was a surprise. The bulimia had almost totally disappeared! Yet, I never once said to Amey, "I'd like to work on my issues with food." She knew I was bulimic because I told her so in the beginning. Instead, she worked on strengthening my core. I never once associated "bio" as a resource to combat bulimia, but that was its effect on me!

Was this a 100% cure? No, but the bulimia was no longer weekly or even monthly. Months would go by with no incident, then once in a blue moon, my inner volcano would erupt, and BOOM! Then many more months would pass! To me, it was a miracle! I'll always be grateful to Amey for her compassion and encouragement. I was glad she charged an affordable price during that time. Today's fee would be a lot more; however, this experience would have been worth it at any price!

29

Forgiving

Dan and I had been married for twelve years when I saw the obituary in the newspaper. I didn't usually read obituaries, but as I was turning the pages, it jumped out at me. Paul had died. I read the details of where and when they would hold the funeral.

On the one hand, I wanted to go. I was dying of curiosity. I wanted to see the other players in this soap opera. Would Louise be there? Likely not, since Paul left her for Linda, their daughter-in-law; probably not Paul's son, Bill, since Linda had left him for his father! I'd also get to see Karen, Paul's daughter, who phoned me on Paul's behalf after our final breakup. And how was Linda holding up? Would there be many people, or only a few? On the other hand, it was not a good idea to attend unless I was invisible.

I could picture myself huddling in the last row of seats in the funeral chapel, listening to the eulogy and the good things well-wishers would say about Paul. Invariably, at the tea afterwards, someone would ask me who I was and how I knew him. "Oh, I was the 'other woman' twenty years ago when he was still married to Louise. Would you please pass the macaroons?"

On the evening of Paul's funeral, Dan went to visit a friend. The evening was mine. I thought that it would be a fitting time to talk to Paul, Gestalt-style. From my reading, I knew that forgiveness plays a major role in spiritual and emotional healing.

A few years earlier, I had successfully used this technique to release the bad feelings between myself and my father. I set up two chairs facing each other. One was my chair; the other represented my dad. I was to play both roles, shifting positions as I spoke first as myself and then as my father. Then I asked God to participate in this forgiveness process.

As my dad, I spoke first. "Beth, why didn't you visit me? I never did anything to you. I worked for you, sent you to a private school, and paid for music lessons. So, how could you just abandon me?"

That part was easy. I told my dad how his alcoholism and his treatment of my mom had affected me. "You don't realize that to a little girl, her mother is a template of the woman she will one day become, and the father is a template of 'all men' and how they treat women. When you were shouting, threatening, and cursing at her, you were shouting, threatening, and cursing at me. When you struck her, you also struck me. I soaked in her fear, agony, and sense of being trapped. Because of your behaviour, I couldn't relate normally to boys when I was a teen, and as a young woman, I was afraid of men.

"I could never relate to you honestly. It's true you never meant to do anything to me—other than the one time I was emotionally honest with you. I was fourteen. You told me to wash my lipstick off; when you told me I looked like a tramp, I blurted out that I hated you. Then you beat me on my shoulders and arms."

"You hurt me deeply when you said that," he replied.

"That's no excuse. I was never able to relate to you honestly because I feared your anger. Everything to you was black and white, and that was that. I always tiptoed on eggshells around you, hypocritical and always 'nice'; God forbid I ever question your authority or express anger toward you. I hated it when Mom said I should apologize to you after the beating, but I did it to go to my job interview. Do you know how that felt? And you never apologized to me for hitting me!"

"I'm sorry. I'm very sorry," said Dad.

I know I said a lot more from my point of view; then, it was my dad's "turn." It was amazing how well I could "get into his skin," so to speak. I realized then how difficult his life had been in many ways. This is what Mom told me shortly after his death.

Michal (Mike) was born post-World War I in Lwow (renamed Lviv, now a part of Ukraine). Bolek, his father, left Magda to live with another woman. In turn, he left Magda with their five children at the time of an extreme food shortage in the city. Mike was the youngest. He remembered Magda bidding the children stay in the house while she was out to search for food. If she were lucky, she'd return with a loaf of black bread, but she often returned empty-handed.

Then one day, Bolek returned, staying only long enough to impregnate his long-suffering wife once again. Then back he went to his mistress.

Magda died of a botched abortion attempt.

Dad was only five years old when Bolek parcelled out his children to various relatives. He then married his lady love. However, Mom never did tell me the rest of that tragic story.

As a young man, Mike joined the Polish army, and soon they were ordered to fight the Germans. The Second World War had wreaked havoc on him. At one point, the authorities assigned Mike to machine gun detail. Dad never got over having killed people and never forgave himself, even though he was just following orders. Shackled by the burden of his guilt, he did not attend mass in later life.

(Here, I should add that shortly before he died, Mom invited a compassionate priest to visit Dad to enable him to make his long overdue confession. Dad was grateful for this opportunity and, hopefully, was able to find some inner peace.)

He was caught three times—once by the Russians and twice by the Germans—taken as a prisoner of war. By hook or by crook, Dad ran off twice, but they recaptured him—he could not escape the third time.

Marrying my mother and fathering three children was the highlight of his life. Dad was determined to give his children the childhood he never had.

Later, Dad watched me draw ever closer to my mother as I approached my preteen years. I wonder if he picked up on the feeling I had as a teenager: that he wasn't very bright, and that Mom had married beneath her. If he did, that must have been very painful. Also, Dad's English was never very good, so, he couldn't express everything he needed or wanted to say beyond a basic level. Unable to communicate with me, he watched me grow further and further away from him. His family meant everything to him, he told me. He loved us, and he was so proud of his smart, beautiful wife and three children. He was proud of his home, and everyone could see that ours was the best, most cultivated yard, and garden in the neighbourhood. He looked after the house immaculately. However, he never could overcome his drinking, and now he realized its impact on me.

"I'm terribly sorry. I love you. I never wanted to hurt you or your mother."

And I felt that; I really did. And I realized that my love for him was still there. I asked for his forgiveness, and he asked for mine.

Our session ended with me saying the "Our Father" out loud in English and "sensing" him saying it in Polish at the same time.

Some years later, after my mother's death, something interesting happened. I'd never dreamed about my father before, but now I dream about my parents frequently together. He is a silent protective figure, watching out for me.

Now in my memories, I have "my good daddy" back—the man who loved small children, made up fantastic stories, built a swing set for me—my daddy who donned a scarf, then knocked at the front door, imitating an old Polish lady we knew. My daddy who baked cakes for the older man who lived alone and an elderly widow, leaving the cakes on their doorsteps, ringing their bells, and running away so they wouldn't know who left the treat. I am grateful that I am able to remember the goodness in him.

I laid to rest the ghosts of my father and the defiant twenty-one-year-old me. I have completely let go of them; may they finally rest in peace.

I decided to use the same procedure with Paul.

Maybe forgiving Paul would help me free up some psychic space. Before proceeding, I said the "Our Father," asking God to be with us in the process. Then, I thoroughly lambasted Paul. I itemized every way he had harmed me, with his manipulations, that godawful "spiritual wedding," his attempts at psychic control and isolating me from my family, and how I had suffered from mental illness and bulimia due to his nefarious influence. Was I ever having a good time! Yeah, sock it to him, baby!

When I moved to the other chair to role-play as Paul, I pictured him cringing.

How very satisfactory it felt! Served the bastard right! At the end of my diatribe, I magnanimously added, "But I forgive you, Paul!"

Was this an example of genuine forgiveness? Nope! However, at the time, I thought, "Job well done!" and patted myself on the back.

30

POSSESSION

About a year later, my sister told me about a psychic healer that she had seen. Eleanor didn't do physical healing, focusing instead on spiritual and emotional healing. So, out of curiosity, I made an appointment with her. Eleanor had me lie down on a massage table.

"We'll start by working on relationships. What happens is that you will picture someone from your past or your present. If you have or have had a positive, loving relationship, you might see a fine gold chain connecting your heart to theirs. That's good. If the relationship was destructive, you might see twine connecting you. You will need to take a large pair of scissors and cut the twine. That will help you let go of the negativity. Now I want you to picture someone, and what it is that binds you."

Guess who I pictured? Yep! Only the picture I imagined was creepy. Extending from the top of my head was a very thick rubbery cord; on the other end, Paul was hanging upside down, with the cord attached to the top of his head. Scissors wouldn't work on that cord! Neither did a knife! Next, I tried gardening shears! Should I have tried with an axe?

I told Eleanor what I saw and how nothing seemed to work. She nodded sagely. "Yes, I can see this man. He's shouting, 'Help! Help!' The cord from the crown of your head to his indicates possession."

"Possession?" I squeaked.

"Yes, and next time I see you, we'll cut you free and put a purple cap on your head for protection."

"I want to make an appointment as soon as possible!"

"I'll be away for the next couple of weeks. Call me then," she said. So casual she was, like a doctor saying, "Take a couple of aspirin and call me in the morning."

But this was POSSESSION, not a cold or a minor headache! EEEW! A couple of weeks? I had to wait that long? I went home in a panic. I couldn't wait that long. Should I go shopping for a purple cap, plonk it on my head, and wear it 24 hours per day until I saw Eleanor again? But then, how would I explain this to Dan? He wouldn't approve of me seeing a psychic—bad idea.

Even though I was the "possessor," not the "possessee," I didn't want to have Paul literally hanging around me forever! Of course, I write in jest, but this was very frightening to me. All I wanted was to move on and live my life and for Paul to move on and live his afterlife, whatever that was to be.

I thought I had dealt with Paul once and for all in my Gestalt session. I'd forgiven him, hadn't I? Then, finally, I realized what I had left out. In Gestalt role-playing, the person you are addressing is supposed to have their say also, whereas I had simply blasted Paul. It was supposed to be a two-way street.

On my next free evening, I set up the chairs. Once again, I said the "Our Father" and asked God to overlook this session.

Paul had a lot to say. Why had I lied to him? I should have taken him seriously about burying the knife! Instead, I had treated it like garbage! He had trusted me, and I had betrayed him! He had given me his heart and soul! I should have just said "no" if I wasn't serious about our "spiritual wedding." Instead, I had been everything to him and I had broken his heart. I had been dishonest throughout our relationship.

Well, now, he wasn't entirely wrong, was he?

In the end, I said I was deeply sorry for hurting him, which I was, and that I hoped we were now mutually free from each other. I wished him the best. He was okay with that, and we forgave each other.

It didn't mean that I condoned his past actions. I simply cut the bonds, setting him and myself free.

That night I had a powerful dream. I dreamed that the cord between Paul and me dissolved completely. A hand reached down from the sky and placed a golden lotus on my head. Then a voice said, "You've given me back my power." It was Paul's voice.

Certainly, this dream resulted in some deep questioning. Did Paul lose his psychic powers because I didn't bury the knife? Was his soul trapped in my aura because of the curse? Or were these images simply a product of my subconscious mind? Of course, I'd never find out. However, I finally realized that these details didn't matter; forgiveness and release were the most important outcomes.

When the two weeks were up, I went back to see Eleanor. I told her what I had done and about the dream of the golden lotus.

She told me she had noticed a shift in my energy as I came in. "You did it!" she said. "You don't need me."

I sauntered out of there like I was the Queen of the Nile. Whoever had crowned me with the lotus had good taste. After all, I'd rather be wearing a golden lotus on my head than some silly purple baseball cap!

I had another dream several nights later—a power dream.

I was back in time living in a former apartment. It was night, and I was looking out the window when I saw Paul's car pull up on the curb. I saw him walk into my building. A short while later, I heard a knock on my door. I didn't open the door.

"Go away, Paul. I didn't invite you here." Without a word, he left. Gazing out the window again, I saw him return to his car and drive away. I felt my own power.

I woke up feeling like, WOW, this is great!

Another power dream followed some time later.

In this dream, the late afternoon sky was gray. Although it was a downtown location, there was no one on the streets. I saw myself walking on the sidewalk. I was wearing a beautiful black coat that I had worn on my European trip. It had black fur cuffs on the sleeves—how I had loved that coat. Although the streets were empty and I was alone, I felt confident and sure of myself. I seemed to know where I was going. I was unafraid. Along the way, I passed a historic brick Presbyterian church, a landmark in our town. End of dream.

I woke up feeling good.

I was free.

31

The Hardest Person in the World to Forgive

For many years, I thought that the hardest person to forgive in my life was Paul. Then, having dealt with that matter as best I could, I thought, "Great! Now I can move on." And I certainly did move on. Yes, I was happy in my marriage, enjoyed my friends, and liked the people I worked with, but I was not happy.

I didn't realize how deeply angry—indeed furious—I was with myself for getting involved with Paul and the resulting self-betrayal. People would say, "It's not your fault; you were innocent. He was your counsellor. You were tricked by a narcissist. The blame lies with him." Nonetheless, that undetected rage siphoned off in an incessant nasty nattering in my head. Without being aware of it, I had a heavy-duty grudge against myself.

"How could I have been so stupid? What's wrong with me? I should have known better!" "I knew he was married! Where were my morals?" "I was such an idiot!" When the bulimia started, it was, "God, I'm disgusting! Who does this?" "What a pig! I'm so weak! Why can't I break this habit?" "I hate myself!" And on and on it went. This self-loathing seeped into my everyday life, and I wasn't even aware of it.

A movie I watched inspired me to change my viewpoint. *Seven Years in Tibet* tells the true story of Heinrich Harrer, an Austrian mountaineer who made his way into Tibet, not an easy feat. There he made friends with the teenage Dalai Lama. During the time he was there, Harrer observed the life and customs of the Tibetan people.

One day, he saw a most curious thing. There was this huge hole in the ground. Someone explained to him that the purpose was to build a foundation for a new building. On every side of the hole, people were kneeling and scooping up handfuls of dirt, which they threw over to the land higher up. What were they doing?

It was explained that these folks were practising the Buddhist principle of "ahimsa," which means "causing no harm to any living being." Yes, that meant even the bugs! So, they were attempting to save every bug they had dug up!

I was watching this and thinking, *Yep, they're saving the lives of bugs that they will later step on during their everyday life! This is an impossible standard!* But then, it struck me. Wasn't I also holding myself to an unattainable standard of perfection?

It began with my early religious training. The church taught me that we are born in original sin and always have to be on the lookout for sinful acts, even thoughts, to confess; mea culpa, mea culpa, mea maxima culpa, which translates to "through my fault, through my fault, through my most grievous fault." As a child in the 1950s, I absorbed all this doom and gloom like a sponge.

Due to the Second Vatican Council (1962 to 1965), the Church has made many positive changes: however, my inner child remained frozen in the fearful fifties.

༄

When I was nine, I was gifted with an autograph book to fill with signatures and well-wishes from family and friends. I remember one poetic gem written by a playmate.

"I saw you in the ocean, I saw you in the sea, I saw you in the bathroom. Ropes, pardon me!" (I think *"ropes"* is supposed to be *"oops"!*)

But I digress. My mother wrote these words.

Be nice, be kind, be sweet, be cute
But most of all, my darling, be good.

When I was in my twenties, I found my autograph book in a heap of stuff I was clearing out. I showed this to Mom, who had since evolved. Her face scrunched up into an expression of supreme distaste. "No! Did I write this? No, no! Don't listen to this nonsense. Be REAL!"

"Too late, Mom," I told her. "You've already ruined me."

For eight years after my spiritual experience, I had lightened up, feeling God loved me exactly the way I was. Then, after the fiasco with Paul, I looped back to the old way of thinking and continued picking on myself.

Junie, my author mentor, listened patiently to my tale of self-disgust with the girl I had been. Then she said, "That same girl who got you into trouble was the one who got you out of it. She caused you to seek and find help. She got you going to university. That girl had guts." The penny dropped. Junie was right.

Now I'm going to share something I did, and it took years to forgive myself.

I had always thought of myself as a kind person who bent over backwards not to hurt another person, but I did.

I was 24 and still dealing with my craziness and the fallout from my relationship with Paul. My new boss wasn't happy with me, my sour face and many mistakes. "SHAPE UP OR SHIP OUT!" he told me bluntly. Panic-stricken, I forced myself to focus on my work. My subsequent review showed much improvement. To get through the workday, I used humour. I wrote funny stories about the staff, one being the results of a men's fashion contest featuring the guys in my office. They loved it, and a few even suggested who else I should include. That was okay.

Now there were two other women in this department—Sherry and Marion. They were very friendly. However, I felt uneasy with them, still smarting from being hurt by Ann and the other women I'd worked with at the previous office.

Soon after, when I wrote a nasty story in the form of a fairy tale about Sherry, it didn't register with me that what I'd written was hurtful. I just thought it was funny. Marion approached me and said, "Sherry thinks you don't like her." I only said, "Oh, no, I like her," and continued typing. Marion's comment should have been my cue to apologize to Sherry, but it simply didn't sink in. I was oblivious. Sherry continued to be friendly with me, bless her. When I finally left that job, I took the stories and poems I'd written and stored them in a scrapbook for future amusement.

I went through that scrapbook about ten years later and came across that story. I was horrified and tore it to pieces. I became fully aware of the bitchy thing I had done. I looked for Sherry in the phone book, thinking I would write a letter of apology, but I couldn't locate her. Much later, when Facebook was born, I tried to look her up with no results. (There were more than thirty people with the same name and surname, and half didn't post any photos of themselves.) Perhaps by now, she had married and used a different surname—another dead end.

I carried my shame about this cruelty until just recently. I worked on it with Cheryl, my spiritual mentor. I told her how ashamed I was all this time and that I still couldn't forgive myself. Cheryl guided me to meditate and go back in time to talk to my 24-year-old self.

"How could you have been so oblivious to the hurt you caused," I asked her. "And you didn't even apologize. That story was vicious!"

The 24-year-old me replied, "I was overwhelmed by my insane thoughts and impulses and the fallout from Paul; I couldn't take anything else in. I was hanging by a thread." I felt the truth of this and was finally able to forgive myself.

Thich Nhat Hanh, a sage and spiritual teacher, explained, *"When a person makes you suffer, it is because he suffers deeply within himself, and his suffering is spilling over. He does not need punishment; he needs help. That's the message he is sending."*

This explanation also made it possible for me to let go of shaming myself over my meanness to Rob and Samir. I wished there was an UNDO button and that I could go back to my earlier years and act with more kindness toward the people I had hurt. However, it is true that my behaviour was motivated by fear. I am now able to look back and have compassion for that nervous, insecure girl.

I held myself to an ideal that I should *never* (ever) hurt anyone. If I deviated from it, that would indicate that I was a mean, rotten person. It is as impossible for me to live up to this standard as it was for the Tibetans not ever to cause harm to an ant. The truth is that occasionally I am a bull in someone's China shop. Also, I can cause hurt feelings when I set boundaries, especially when the other person doesn't like what I say. Nonetheless, I do need to speak up.

The magic phrase for me is "I am human." As humans, we are fallible and prone to error. Yes, even me at age 70 plus!

Saying, "I am human," is a more compassionate way to view myself. I take responsibility for my actions, make amends where possible, and forgive myself.

If I can't make direct amends to someone, I make sure I'll never repeat the action. I'm happy to say that I have never written a hurtful story again.

My self-talk has changed. Whenever I go back to my "default setting" of self-castigation, I now counter it by listing the good things I have done. After all, as fallible as we humans are, we also do some wonderful deeds and are capable of great kindness.

I must tell you what happened on the day when I wrote this chapter. A friend and I met for lunch. She said to me, "You look beautiful," to which I replied, "Oh, but I hate my frown lines. They make me look as if I'm always in a bad mood."

Then she said, "I never even noticed them, but now I do."

We both laughed.

Why did I do that? I sabotaged a lovely compliment! Jeez, when will I ever learn to say, "thank you" and allow myself to feel great that someone thought I looked beautiful? Ah, well, practice, practice, practice!

Now I am beginning to compliment myself. I'll try to make this a regular thing.

I should tell you that a domestic diva, I am not, and I hate vacuuming. I postpone, postpone, and postpone. Finally, a few weeks ago, I couldn't stand looking at my carpets full of dirt, crumbs, and cat hair. Grumpily, I finally applied myself to this loathsome task, swearing as I did so at the poor vacuum, which surely didn't deserve this verbal abuse.

I complimented myself all day long. "Wow! Aren't I great? The floor looks so clean! Look what I did! Whoopee! Good for me!"

Does that seem trivial? It isn't. Celebrate your small, everyday accomplishments, as well as your significant achievements. Celebrate yourself! You're worth it!

32

COLLAGE

My Life in Bits and Pieces

My life since Dan's death spreads out on the wall—a ten-year collage in bits and pieces. There is no theme, just snapshots of various moods and hues; an honest collage, not like Facebook, where I endeavour to jazz up my posts to prove to others that I am always happy, happy, happy. Oh, yes, I have happy pictures in my collage, but the darker ones are there for balance.

I'll begin with a bleak-looking portrait covering two years—Dan's unexpected death from a heart attack that ended his life and shattered mine. In the meantime, while I was in that state of mind, I had tons of paperwork to deal with since I was the executor of Dan's Will. I sought out a psychiatrist and subsisted on Citalopram, an antidepressant, Trazodone, a sleeping pill, and Clonazepam (a tranquilizer), and not much else. With the help of the tranquilizer, I took two naps a day.

Reality felt like too much to cope with for ages. Eventually, I weaned myself from the Clonazepam.

According to Reader's Digest and other sources, my grieving was supposed to end in six months. Also, an intern told me the same thing, so they must teach this nonsense in medical school. However, in my case, it took two years for my intense mourning to soften, as it did for several other widows who I spoke with around that time. Grief doesn't really "end," but eventually we are able to make a new life for ourselves. It was a relief to know I wasn't the only one unable to stick to the prescribed timeline!

A somewhat brighter image shows my move to a neighbourhood where I always wanted to live. My condo is one block from the ocean and a few blocks from a beautiful park. My brother, Ray, and his lovely wife, Vana, really came through for me in helping with the move. Ray was a realtor and sold my house quickly at a good price. Lita, my sister, provided a sturdy shoulder for me to cry on. She was my constant support. I'll always be grateful to them and the friends who helped me during that chaotic time. There are gray areas in this picture also. It took me almost a year to adjust to living alone once again, so alone and lonely, and so utterly missing Dan.

Now, here I am in a charity thrift store where I volunteer. See me combing through the racks for size eight clothing. Size 8! During my time of grieving, I lost 35 pounds with no effort. Food? Who wants food when the love of your life has passed away? Not even chocolate, ice cream, or pastries enticed me.

I enjoy my volunteer work. Everyone is lovely and friendly, and I get to know people in my community. The other volunteers are fun to work with, too. I'm still volunteering there in my tenth year.

Alas! My appetite returned with a vengeance, and I've blossomed into a bountiful size 16!

Oooh! I think there's a guy who's interested in me. I met him in my church. He approached me rather flirtatiously and asked if I would go for coffee with him. Well, why not? Came the day, and there I was, sitting in a local hangout. George was sitting across from me, regaling me about the business he had set up, investing in volcanic ash—the most fertile soil to grow plants. This monologue took up the bulk of our time. I was surprised when he asked me for a second coffee date.

He brought a briefcase and extracted some papers, which he placed on the table. Would I be interested in investing in volcanic ash for $1,000.00, maybe even $2,000.00? I'd get a super good rate of return. He showed me a contract. "Thanks, but no thanks!"

I invited a man to meet me for coffee. I thought, *nothing ventured, nothing gained.* But, although we didn't click, we remained friendly.

There was also a fellow with whom I'd been making eye contact.

He asked me out for a coffee date. I knew it wouldn't work when he inquired if I had ever walked from my neighbourhood to a beach many kilometers away.

"Uh, no."

"What do you do to keep fit?" he asked.

Gulp! "Reading, writing, napping, and watching Netflix?"

He disapproved.

So much for late-life romance!

In the past eleven years, I have become independent and set in my ways. Do I really want to adjust to some guy cluttering up my apartment and criticizing my bad habits? Lately, the biggest romance in my life is with my cat!

⚭

Sasha, my beautiful kitty, reminds me that there is still joy in life. I saw her photo on "Kijiji," which advertises everything from A to Z for sale. She is dark gray with white feet and white markings on her belly. Her former owners loved Sasha and didn't want to give up their precious three-year-old. However, living with six kids and three dogs was too much for her. The third dog disliked her, and the feeling was mutual. Sasha spent months cowering under the bed. The owners consulted with the veterinarian and sought advice from an animal behaviour therapist. However, Sasha wouldn't budge. Finally, both the vet and the therapist recommended a new home for her. This situation wasn't good for her mental health.

When Janine brought her to me, she admitted ruefully that her place was a zoo! As soon as she let Sasha out of the carrier, she ran directly to hide under my bed (Sasha, not Janine). I expected the cat would stay there for some time before getting used to me, but do you know what? As soon as Janine left, out she came. Sasha ran all around the living room, down the hall, and back to the living room. Occasionally, she jumped on my lap to cuddle, purring loudly. She ran, and she ran, and she ran. I've never seen such pure joy in an animal!

Sasha has been with me for two years now. She has the sweetest temperament and shows her love by massaging my tummy and licking my hand. Sasha enjoys visitors; she flops on her back to show off her considerable belly.

For your information, I do go for walks, especially in spring and summer. I stroll through my neighbourhood, taking in the sights—the trees, the flowers, the ocean, and old Victorian houses, some designated as heritage. I keep stopping. "Oh! Look at this! Look at that!" I walk an hour or two each day.

Yes, that's me in the spotlight. I'm wearing a ruby-red wig and people laugh at my jokes (all my own material!). So, how did this come about?

It happened at the Easter service in my church. I should inform you that The Church of Truth is not a conventional one. They invited me to be the Easter bunny; I sure had fun wearing the requisite bunny ears and telling my story. Back in the garden of Eden, God told me, the first bunny, to be fruitful and multiply. I was happy to oblige, but, of course, I needed a mate. Then along came Bugs Bunny, wooing me with 24 carrots, and I have been prolific ever since!

Diana, a professional comedian, happened to be attending that service. Once a month, she coordinated a comedy show at a coffee house. She invited local comedians to take part. Diana enjoyed my performance and—presto! There I was. I performed several times until Diana was unable to continue with the show.

Undaunted, I signed up for a comedy class with other wannabe comedians. Our "graduation" was at the same coffee house and we each had an opportunity to show our stuff. I was delighted at how it went for me and had a great response to my story about my date with a ninety-year-old billionaire.

Ah, this picture is not so happy. I'm at Connect Hearing for a hearing test once again. The news is not great. I've had moderate hearing loss for years; now, the range veers from moderate to severe. Mind you, volume alone does not restore my hearing. My brain is sometimes slow to process incoming messages. How well I hear also depends on the voice quality of the person speaking. I don't do well with soft voices or heavy accents. Some people get irritated with me and ask when I had my last hearing test. It was just a few months ago if you really want to know.

On the lighter side, some of my mishears are funny. For example, at a pub, I saw a woman I haven't seen for a few years.

"What have you been up to, Joan?"

"Last week, I talked to a horse," she replied.

I wondered what the horse had to say. Actually, Joan had signed up for a course that week.

Here's another doozy. Lita told me that her favourite program was *Pit Bulls and Perogies,* to which I replied, "You take the pit bulls, and I'll go for the perogies." I'm sure you can guess the word was really "parolees."

Sad to say, I broke off with a friend of forty-five years. Our formerly close friendship gradually morphed into an unhealthy pattern. I grew nervous in her presence. If I brought up an issue, she would yell at me. At first, I felt I should remain loyal to her as ours was a long-term relationship. However, my first loyalty is to myself and my sanity. At my age, I need peaceful and respectful relationships—and so, "goodbye"; but I do remember our earlier good times, and I wish her well.

Oh YUCK! COVID, in all its multiple forms and mutations, blights our lives! It was unsettling when malls, small stores, businesses, and restaurants had to shut down. Standing in line at the supermarket—six feet apart—felt weird, as if I was in the Twilight Zone. In a panic, shoppers had stripped some of the shelves of their goods—especially toilet paper. You could get arrested for going the wrong way down the aisles! Well, almost.

Then we had to wear masks. The bane of my life is the masks. As a hard-of-hearing person, I found it twice as hard to understand people wearing masks. I need to see a person's whole face so I can lip read. Thank goodness we have a reprieve from wearing masks, but who knows for how long?

I am distressed by the animosity displayed by "anti-vaxxers" toward "vaxxers," and vice versa. I pray that all this division will be over soon.

There is a saying on Facebook: *"We're all in the same storm but not in the same boat! Some have yachts, some have canoes, and some drown."*

My boat is a sturdy vessel somewhere in between a yacht and canoe, and, so far, it is staying afloat. My heart goes out to families with children, all who have lost their jobs and businesses, and those who endured further physical abuse when ordered to stay home.

"Bless you all, whatever the size of your boat, and may all of us survive the storm and live a freer, happier life when we reach the shore."

According to Wikipedia, synchronicity is "the simultaneous circumstances that appear meaningfully related yet lack a causal connection." What a mouthful that is!

In my case, I was talking to a friend on the phone. I told her I felt like God had forgotten me.

Now, right at that time, Junie was walking along a beach. She gasped. "Oh my God! I can't believe what I'm seeing." She described a rock wall on which was printed (in chalk), "Beth," followed by the drawing of a heart, "I love you." And then, she said, breathlessly, "And it's signed 'God!'"

"Are you serious? You're not just saying that to make me feel better?"

"Here, I'll take a photo of it and send it to your email."

Sure enough, there it was in the photo, although I had doubts about the signature, which was a little faded. Yes, it was only three letters, and the middle one was an O, but was that first letter a G or an R? And the last letter; was it a B or a D? Could it be Rob or Rod? Hard to make out. I expressed my doubts to Junie.

Well, she took me firmly in hand. "Beth, you have a choice. You can choose to accept it as a positive message for you and feel better or continue to feel miserable. The timing is uncanny."

It certainly was, so I decided to accept this message as meant for me.

Five years earlier, I was walking downtown when a little piece of rose-pink construction paper caught my eye. It had a heart drawn on it. Curious, I picked it up. It was a pocket-sized card. When I opened it, the message read: "You've got what it takes to do whatever you want!" As it was unaddressed, I decided this card was meant for me. Of all the people pounding the city pavements, I was the one to discover it. I still have it!

Now I'm looking for these small messages from the universe as signs that I'm on the right path. They give me great comfort.

On and on I go. It's true what they say about old age not being for sissies as the symptoms pile up—osteoarthritis in my right knee, a tremor in my right hand, and various aches and pains.

Most difficult to bear is the death of family members and many good friends. I go to more memorial services than weddings these days!

Stefan, Mom's partner, died in 2005 of brain cancer. After a long struggle with Leukemia, my mother passed in 2007. Four years later, Dan's heart gave out.

These losses have made me feel very vulnerable. My significant others are no longer here to shield me, and now I am the oldest person in my family. How many years do I have left?

However, my life is still good. During the past two years, I have taken an author mentorship course on Zoom, which has enabled me to write this book. I'm also "zooming" with my spiritual mentor to take care of my inner life using her powerful meditations. These courses have kept me sane during this sad time.

I still believe in God but not as defined and confined in any holy book or religion. This God is neither a "He" nor "She," more a Consciousness that embraces and inhabits the cosmos with its multiverses and the tiniest bit of matter. I call it The Great Mystery! I'm with Einstein when he tells us we are like small children in a vast library, creeping about in awe as we look around. The library was there long before we were.

I believe God reaches out to us in many ways, according to our understanding. For example, the spiritual awakening that I experienced when I was a believing Catholic is still sacred to me. It is my foundation and what started me on a positive spiritual path. Although I have parted ways with the Catholic faith, I continue to connect with my personal God as I experience Him. He lives in my heart always.

Have I finally "arrived"? Arrived where? I used to think that by the time I was this old, I would sail through life ever calm and serene and that nothing would upset me again. I have two words to say to that—HA and HA! Perhaps the purpose of my journey is the journey itself and learning to roll with the punches. And maybe the biggest gain would be to see the beauty in my surroundings, myself, and other people more consistently, even as I walk through the chaos!

I've never returned to being the naive, overly optimistic young woman I was. However, now I know that with the help of my Higher Power and the support of loving, positive people, I can deal with whatever comes up.

I am grateful to my Big Bad Wolf for enabling me to discover my own strength, resilience, and power.

33

Advice from a Crone

*R*ed Riding Hood's Grandma was looking forward to the weekly visit from her beloved grandchild. However, arthritis and a bad case of diarrhea mean she didn't get out much and spent much of her day in bed. Red Riding Hood would bring special herbal teas, yummy vegan tofu broccoli raisin squares, and horse liniment to rub on her aching joints.

At last, there was a knock on her door, and a figure arrayed in a bright red and white checked tablecloth pranced up to her bed. On top of its head sat a large red woollen tea cozy.

"Good morning, Grandma!" it said in a deep croaky voice.

Grandma felt a twinge of apprehension. It sounded almost—masculine. "Your voice sounds so hoarse. Have you caught a cold, sweetie?"

"No, Grandma dear, it must be your poor hearing."

"Could be," Grandma muttered to herself. She was way overdue for a hearing test. Even so, something felt off.

"My goodness, child, how tall you've grown!"

"Yes, thanks to Uncle Jack's magic beans."

"Hmm." Still, wasn't six-foot-four a little tall for a 14-year-old? "But what happened to your face? It's so hairy!"

"Grandma, have you lost your eyeglasses again?"

Now Grandma was getting suspicious. She wasn't a stupid woman. She'd been around the block a few times. "I have a special gift for you—my diamond necklace and a small bag of gold, but I've put it in the root cellar for safekeeping. Would you please fetch it for me?"

The wolf stopped in mid-drool. "A diamond necklace, you say?"

"Yes, my dear. And the gold also! The trap door is in the kitchen under the table."

The wolf took off like a shot.

Hastily, Grandma jumped out of her bedroom window and ran off to who knows where! She was very spry for an old lady.

The wolf spent quite some time moving the heavy table and looking for the non-existent trap door. In a fury, he ran back into the bedroom to gobble up the old lady. Then, when he found that she had tricked him, he howled and howled and howled. But, oh well, old bones make poor meat.

Anticipating Red's visit, the wolf quickly tore off his disguise and jumped under the covers. Just in time, he donned one of Grandma's nightcaps. Then, hearing a knock on the door, he grinned a wolfish grin and greeted the precious little granddaughter!

I won't bore you. If you've read the story, you know how that conversation went. Oh, Grandma, what big eyes, nose, teeth you have, blah, blah, blah.

Surveying his next feast—what a dish! —the wolf started to slobber, drool running down his chin. Then, just as he was about to spring— Grandma flew into the bedroom with her friend, the woodcutter. As the woodcutter raised his axe, the wolf started to whimper.

"I'm just a poor boy from a poor family. When I was just a cub, my dad ran off with some bitch. Then a few months later, a hunter shot my mama! When I was full-grown, I hunted him down. I was starving, and, well, he was my first. Never did like venison, anyhow."

"Don't you dare bloody my nice clean sheets," Grandma whispered to her friend.

Sighing, the woodcutter handed the axe over to grandma and pulled out a pair of handcuffs, for he doubled as the village sheriff, you see. He had brought a muzzle specifically for this occasion, which he fastened onto the nose and mouth of the whimpering wolf. A chain-linked leash with an iron collar made it impossible for the offender to escape.

That nasty critter was exiled to Siberia, far, far away from any human dwelling. Who knows what happened to him.

As for Red and Grandma, they lived safely and happily ever after.

Take a lesson from Grandma. She felt uneasy; something was off. She trusted her instincts.

She then had the presence of mind to trick the wolf and escape to get help. Because she listened to her feelings, she saved both her life and her precious granddaughter. On the other hand, Red simply stood rooted to the spot and gaped at the wolf. She even passed him a Kleenex to wipe the drool off his face. She didn't trust her perceptions. (Maybe Grandma *had* grown hair on her face and had a dental problem that caused those teeth to grow into fangs.) Luckily, Grandma charged in at just the right time with the woodcutter.

Was Red stupid? No, she was simply inexperienced. Was I stupid? No, I was in the same boat as Red. When I started out in my adult life, I was like a baby duck. I still needed to follow the lead of people I felt were wiser or more authoritative than me. I didn't know that the deepest source of wisdom is within myself, my gut instincts, my doubts, my feelings, and my intuition. God gave me a brain, but it took me many years to learn how to use it!

Luckily, I am now a "crone," matured with age, a little wisdom, and a ton of therapy.

So now, let me share some of the lessons I learned in the school of hard knocks!

Let us review the chapter entitled "Love Declared."

Immediately after I confessed to Paul that I'd fallen in love with him, he was ready for action. "How can we be together?" he mused. The responsible thing for him to do as a counsellor was to explain that what I was feeling was transference, which occurs in a therapeutic relationship when a client transfers their feelings to the therapist. When Paul, as my counsellor, recognized that transference was taking place for both of us, he should have backed away and given me a referral to another counsellor.

Goodness, gracious! The guy was *married,* AND they had "a beautiful marriage," or so he said. He told me he would never divorce his wife. Now here was a recipe for trouble! Ah, foolish girl that I was, I thought I could "borrow" Paul for a short while, and then leave to resume my life path. Such was my youthful illusion!

Commandment:
Thou shalt not borrow
another woman's husband!
He is not for rent!

In "Gifts," Paul's actions further indicated that not all was right in my romance. I had precisely described what I wanted in full detail. *"Anything you want, darling!" he told me.* Instead, Paul brought something completely different, attributing negative characteristics to my desired Geisha doll. *"So stiff and cold; not like you at all."* He insulted my taste and imposed his wishes over mine. *"This is what you wanted, isn't it, darling?"* His misperception (deliberate?) of my desire was a HUGE warning sign.

In Latin, there is a saying,
"de gustibus non est disputandum."
It means "there is no arguing about taste."
You have a right to your taste;
no one should override it with their notion of
what they consider to be more pleasing.
"This is what you wanted,
isn't it, darling?"
HELL NO!

What can I say about "A Wedding and Two Curses"? Paul did describe the ceremony for our "spiritual wedding" a few days earlier. I felt deeply uneasy. What did curses have to do in a celebration of love and joy at committing to each

195

other? I wasn't even ready to commit. Imagine the trouble that would have been prevented had I said, "No, I'm not ready for that." But I didn't know how to say those words. Saying "no" was scary and would hurt people or make them angry. It was easier for me to comply.

During the ceremony, I felt queasy, later going to bed with a splitting headache and nausea. My body was saying, "No, no, no, no!" although I had already said "Yes." I was Echo following her Narcissus. (Remember the myth?)

> ***Do not ever take part in any ritual***
> ***that involves cursing yourself***
> ***or another person.***
> ***You might take it lightly,***
> ***but your subconscious mind does not.***

In "Psychic Experiments," Paul demonstrated that he did have some genuine psychic power. For example, when we were in my bed one time, he suddenly roused and instructed me to hurry and get dressed. "Your friend across the hall is curious about me. She's coming over with the excuse of returning the pot that she borrowed from you." Shortly, there was a knock on the door. It was Rosie, pot in hand!

Then, sometime later, Paul said he needed to nap on my couch. He closed his eyes, and suddenly started to speak. None other than St. Peter introduced himself as Paul's guardian. Supposedly, my guardian was Joan of Arc. *Really?* I wondered. *Hmmm. What would a saint of that stature want with me?*

A friend of mine once went to see a psychic who said her guardian was some guy named "George," without the "Saint." That made far more sense to me!

Just because a person
has some psychic power
doesn't mean that everything
he says is true.

Do not take every message
as the word of God!
It is all too easy for a Big Bad Wolf
to manipulate you through
so-called psychic revelations!

In "My Mother was My Love Rival," Paul insinuated himself into my family by giving gifts and accepting dinner invitations; Mom took this as a sign that he was in love with her. She was delighted, as she, too, had fallen for him. I couldn't tell her that Paul had already chosen to be with me! This situation drove a wedge between Mom and me.

A Big Bad Wolf sows
dissension and confusion
in your family and close relationships.

"DANGER FROM THE EAST!" I wanted counselling in the first place to stop hurting guys who didn't deserve it. In this chapter, my admirer, Samir, recited a poem dedicated to me. I start to melt. While Paul and I didn't have a legal ceremony, I did feel "committed." When I told Paul what had occurred, he said, "Let's see what your guardian says." St. Joan was frantic. "THERE IS DANGER! DANGER FROM THE EAST!" Paul then told me I should tear up Samir's poem and mail it back to him.

Paul was jealous.
It certainly wasn't St. Joan shouting,
"DANGER FROM THE EAST!"

Don't be like me!
You don't have to do everything
your wolf says, especially
if it involves hurting other people.

In the chapter entitled "Exile," Paul and I were almost caught by Mom, Lita, and Ray *in flagrante* when they dropped in on me. Immediately, Paul stressed the importance of not getting caught. *"It could ruin my reputation, darling. I could lose my job."* We then agreed that I should move much farther from my family and friends.

Neither of us considered the effect
of this move on me;
how isolated I would feel
cut off from the people I loved most
and my consequent loneliness
because of our secrets.
Paul had isolated me
both physically and emotionally.

If your Big Bad Wolf
panics about getting caught,
it is because he knows
he is doing something wrong.
He doesn't deserve your protection.
You need to take care of yourself
first and foremost.

In "My Ordeal," Paul did an about-face. I believe he saw how miserable I was and feared he was losing his hold on me. Therefore, he wanted me to prove my love for him by meeting him at my centrally located workplace twice a week for lunch. In spite of my premonition that this plan would have severe consequences, I reluctantly agreed.

I was isolated from my family and friends,
and, in the end, I was the one who lost
my reputation and (almost) my job!

"A Sad, Bad End" shows my tipping point. I couldn't take any more of the loneliness, isolation, and being picked on by the office gossips, and I finally found the courage to break off with him. Although Paul told me that the ultimate author-ity (God) demanded that we stay together, I listened to my feelings and stuck to my guns. I had finally found my voice.

I thought this would be the final break-up, but it wasn't. As I wrote in "Boomerang," Paul was still present in my life. Whenever Mom invited me for supper, Paul was there, taking on the role of "Pater Familias," being his most charming self. There was still a powerful attraction between us, so I decided to give him a second chance. At least I had progressed enough to set some conditions.

> *It takes whatever it takes for us*
> *to decide on our own best interests.*
> *Sometimes the lesson needs to be*
> *repeated before we finally "get it."*

In "The Second Time Around," the first thing I learned in Al-Anon was that we need to take care of ourselves *first!* Even with all that support, the relationship still didn't work out.

The breaking point was when Paul told me he wanted to divorce his wife and then asked me to marry him for real this time. That's when I realized that things had gone too far. That's when I broke off with him for the final time.

Paul still wanted to get me back and asked his daughter to phone me to plead his case, which is "triangulating," two people pitted against one, another form of attempting to control.

> *If your Big Bad Wolf convinces a third*
> *person to convince you to return to him,*
> *don't be intimidated.*
> *The third party doesn't know your side*
> *of your story. Stick to your guns!*

Now we come to "MADNESS—Scenes from an Unquiet Mind." Wouldn't you think that now when I did the "right thing," my life would resume its formerly sunny pace?

It's hard enough to break up from a "normal" relationship. However, nothing about the "bad romance" between Paul and me was "normal." I spiralled downward and continued to do so for the next few years. Nowadays, that would be called *post-traumatic stress.*

Also, my subconscious mind downloaded its earlier programming from our "spiritual wedding" with its two curses, *"Oh, yeah! Beth said if she ever left this guy, may she be killed by a knife. Okay. And she also said, 'May I be unhappy for the rest of my life.' DONE!"*

Be careful how you program
your subconscious mind,
and remember you are more than
your past programming.
You don't have to stay stuck.

In "Looking for Help in All the Wrong Places"—yes, it took some time for me to find the help I needed. It didn't work for me when I sought out regular "talk about it" counsellors. I felt in my gut that I needed something more potent, only I didn't know what that would be. Desperately, I took myself to the Mental Health office to talk to a psychiatrist. Maybe I needed to be committed. She was a haughty woman who told me I was trying to ditch my responsibilities and only looking for attention. I knew that woman was wrong and that I did need help, but where to go?

After I visited with that psychiatrist, I was at an all-time low. If ever there was a point when I would have tried to die by suicide, that was it, but like the Energizer Bunny, I kept going—long after all the other batteries died out. Remember that commercial?

*It might be a while before you find the
"right fit" in counselling or therapy.
Keep on trying. You're worth it!*

In "AHA! PHOBIC NEURRROTIC!" my old buga-boos returned with a vengeance. *It was the devil causing my scary thoughts and impulses!* Even though I knew this was irrational, I developed a morbid fear of "devil possession."

Finally, I fled to the local hospital and started crying at the nurses' desk. The nurse on duty called a psychiatrist to see me. His diagnosis made me laugh. Predictably, he prescribed Valium the drug of the '70s. After a five-day assessment in the mental health ward, I was sent home. Fearing potential addiction, I threw out the valium.

Looking back on my search for sanity from 1972 to 1976, I empathize with the girl who chose to "rough it" without pharmaceutical help. Presently, I do take antidepressants when necessary and they have helped me on the few occasions that I needed them.

However, medication alone doesn't solve all my problems. Whenever I need extra support, I seek a counsellor of therapist to gain insight into what I am going through. I have also found help by joining support groups with people who are going through something similar.

Take prescription drugs when necessary
but do seek out other sources of help.
Support groups can be especially beneficial.

That's it for going chapter by chapter; now, I will make some notes. As you know, I finally found help, which helped me heal. I discovered that I needed therapy that would help me safely vent my emotions *physically*. Both Gestalt and Bioenergetics worked for me.

You don't have to copy what I did
in your search for sanity.
There is no one-size-fits-all therapy.
That means discovering what works for you.

I have read about people who can forgive instantly—just like that! For example, I read about a man whose wife had been killed in an accident by a drunk driver. He forgave the driver right away!

I have a deep admiration for people who can do that. However, I am not one of them. As a people-pleaser, I stored up a lot of grudges. I needed to acknowledge and respect my long-repressed hurt and anger.

When you hold on to hurt and hatred, you keep reliving your trauma long after your offender is gone. Why would you do that to yourself? When you forgive, you free yourself from the chains that bind you.

Forgiving doesn't mean that you condone whatever happened to you, and you don't have to see that person ever again. It's saying, "You go your way, and I'll go mine." It is a way of "letting go" and finding inner peace.

If you find yourself unable to forgive your wolf, it is crucial to stop recycling the endless shame/blame game. Seek extra help to find another way to free yourself.

> *Let go of the past and leave space*
> *for positive feelings to fill your soul.*
> *Then, you can enjoy your life again.*

Self-forgiveness—now that's a toughie—and it's vital to your mental health. Are your standards set too high, like mine were? How is your self-talk? Become a friend to yourself, loving and compassionate.

> *Don't hold yourself hostage—the price is too high!*
> *Give yourself permission to be free.*

Life frequently throws us curve balls like the present pandemic. In Lynn Anderson's song "I Never Promised You a Rose Garden," she sings, "Along with the sunshine, you've got to get a little rain sometime."

This line reminds me of a story that a friend of my mother's told me about Mom. Gloria was sitting at Mom's kitchen table, bewailing her problems. They seemed endless. Then she stopped complaining and asked, "Eva, when will this ever stop?" Mom intoned in a sepulchral voice, "IN THE GRRRAVE!" That was Mom for you!

A friend was discouraged, sitting on a log at the beach near her place. She'd lost her job, she was going through a painful and expensive divorce, and her teenage son was acting up. She said to herself, "Oh well, at least things can't get any worse." At that precise moment, a seagull flew over her and shit on her head! She had to laugh. (She is doing fine now in her new job and her new life, but it took a few years to resolve her problems.)

If you don't expect perfection,
you won't be disappointed.
However, once you learn how
to heal from your trauma,
you can deal with almost
anything life throws at you.

As challenging as I may sometimes find it to do, I try to notice the beauty surrounding me—trees, flowers, clouds in the sky, and the beach with the quiet swish of waves. I think of the good times I've had—with my loving husband, family, friends, parties, travels, and many happy experiences, and I am grateful.

Gratitude is so important.
It reminds us that we're not
victims or emotional paupers.
We see our strengths and the
richness of our lives.
Gratitude gives us balance
and perspective when the bad times come.

Thank you for sharing in my personalized soap opera. Sometimes truth is stranger than fiction. If you are or have been in a similar situation, know that you are not alone. It may take some time, but I believe you can find that life is beautiful once again. I believe in you!

I wish you love, joy, and strength.
Above all,
I wish you a deep and
abiding inner peace.

Acknowledgments

Without the continual support of my "tribe," writing this book would have been a daunting and lonely task. They say that it takes a village to raise a child, which also holds true for a budding writer.

I wish to thank Junie Swadron, my author mentor, for her invaluable input and encouragement for the two years we worked together to bring this book into being. Whenever I grew discouraged and questioned whether I should continue writing, Junie donned her "psychotherapist's hat" and rejuvenated my spirit.

I am also grateful to Becky Norwood of Spotlight Publishing House, for her wisdom, patience, and gentle guidance. Becky did everything she could to ensure that my work with her was a comfortable and enjoyable experience. She truly is the publisher with a heart.

It has been a pleasure to work with Lynn Thompson, my editor. Lynn went beyond sifting through my manuscript to edit grammar, spelling, and punctuation. She also collaborated with me to clarify my writing by recommending additional descriptions in some chapters, making better word choices, and effectively moving some paragraphs into a new order. Lynn's care and attention to detail made my manuscript the best it could be. I would welcome the opportunity to work with her again. Also, Lynn knows all the words for "I Don't Know How to Love Him."

Cheryl Stelte, my spiritual mentor, has helped me immensely with her powerful healing meditations and her faith in my abilities.

I'd like to express my gratitude to Amey Lariviere for leading me through a process (Bioenergetics) that has been crucial to my emotional recovery.

I'm deeply grateful to Al-Anon and their twelve-step program for providing me with a solid spiritual base as well as with several wise "sponsors" to guide me through the steps.

To my friend, Esther Hart, a thank you for reading my manuscript and for writing an endorsement of my work.

Thank you to my family and friends who encouraged me to write this book.

About the Author

Elizabeth **Brown** wrote her first story when she was seven years old. Ever since then, she has written poems, stories, and more than 30 songs.

For three years, Elizabeth volunteered at the NEED Crisis Line, where she learned to listen to callers compassionately and non-judgmentally. Later, she graduated from Notre Dame University with a Bachelor of Arts in Theatre and English.

Her various jobs—clerical, market research, and retail, in addition to research and writing for special projects—have given her a wide range of experience. Eventually, she found long-term employment with the Provincial Government.

Now retired, she relishes the opportunity to pursue her passion for writing. For ten years, Elizabeth has volunteered in a charity thrift shop where she enjoys getting acquainted with people in her community. She has also dabbled in stand-up comedy.

Having recovered from a toxic relationship, Elizabeth wishes to offer hope and encouragement to women in similar straits.

Elizabeth lives in Canada on beautiful Vancouver Island.